15 Minutes with Jesus

15 Minutes with Jesus

with

Mark Hikes

ISBN 978-1-934817-53-7

by Mark Hikes

10 9 8 7 6 5 4 3 2 1

First Edition

Great American Publishers

171 Lone Pine Church Road • Lena, MS 39094

TOLL-FREE 1.888.854.5954 • www.GreatAmericanPublishers.com

To purchase books in quantity for church groups,
corporate use, incentives, or fundraising, please call
Great American Publishers at 888-854-5954.

Attention Youth Leaders, if you use this with your group,
we would love to hear from you. Call or text Mark Hikes with
your feedback or to talk about having him visit your youth group.
(717) 439-8575 or mhhikes@gmail.com.

TABLE OF CONTENTS

DEDICATION

~~~~~~~~~

I dedicate this book to my students in our family group. Your engagement on our Christian journey inspires me to be the best I can be for you. Thank you!

To my wife Natalie and sons, DJ and Jack—this book would not be possible without your love and support. I love US! I love the time we spend together with Jesus. Thank you for all you do!

READER COMMENTS

This book takes every day ideas and feelings that we all know and ties it in to scripture with different ways to think about how God uses it in our lives.

†**Elizabeth**

This text is the first thing that I read when I wake up. My first notification on my phone. I open the message and start off my day like this every morning. It's an honor to be the first ones to read this great message of God from Mark. It gets me through the day. And I can't wait for y'all to start every morning just like I do because believe me you won't regret it!

†**Alexa**

This book made me really think about my time spent with Jesus and how important fifteen minutes can be to your faith.

†**Lindsey**

Getting the text in the morning helps me start my day off positively. It has also helped me stay focused on God throughout these crazy times!

†**Kathryn**

This book helped me so much with my walk with Christ. It kept me thinking about all the great things that come with being a Christian. It was something I could lean on for advice and verses. This book made me more aware with what I was doing and helped me do more good for others. I'm so glad I was able to read this.

†**Jake**

If there is anything in the world worth being head over heels about, it is being loved by, knowing, loving, and following the God we meet in the face of Jesus Christ. Mark gets that to the deepest core of his being. He wants that for you and every person he meets or reaches. It has been my pleasure to spend quality time with Mark over the last couple of years as I have seen him grow. His faith in, and witness for, Christ have challenged and shaped me and many others. Jesus has rescued him and changed everything. Mark wants to put his arm around you as a deep soul friend and walk together into an ever-growing intimacy with the One who loves each of us most. There really is nothing better or more important in life. The insights that Jesus is breathing into Mark through His Word and by His Spirit will help you take the first or next step in this relationship with Jesus that will last for all eternity. Do yourself the greatest of favors—be sure to set aside 15 minutes as often as possible each day to get to know "the One and Only Son who came from the Father, full of grace and truth" (John 1)!

†Ben Butler, Associate Pastor, Madison United Methodist

I've always been told to listen to people I aspire to be like one day. The man that wrote this book is one of those people. He exemplifies commitment, humbleness, and truth through both his actions and his words and I cannot thank him enough for reminding us daily how loved we are.

†Kate

The book gives me a new thought each day. It has helped me build a stronger relationship with Christ.

†Julia Lee

This book allows you to be with God even when you feel like you can't. It allows me to reflect on my relationship with Christ. It is a start to eternity with God and has helped me focus more on Him. This book is everything I didn't know I needed.

†Genna

Have you ever seen a group that you wanted to approach but were hesitant? Then someone says, "Hey, come join us!" Mark is that someone, and this book is his invitation. If you've wanted to start or strengthen your relationship with Jesus, Mark wants to walk with you. His words are warm, wise, reassuring, and often funny and light. Accept his invitation; you won't regret it.

†Liz Howell Pritchard, Mentor Partner

Fifteen minutes with Jesus has taught me the importance of spending time in the Word. The book has brought me close to Jesus. I look forward to reading it every day.

†Doug Owens, Mentor Partner

I have been blessed to serve with Mark in student ministry. I've witnessed a tentative "yes" when he was first asked to serve, grow into a deep desire to see students enter into a lasting and thriving relationship with Jesus Christ. This book is evidence of his passion to see people develop as followers of Jesus. What a simple yet effective way to grow spiritually...15 minutes with Jesus.

†Cory Phillips, Youth Pastor, Madison United Methodist

I have been blessed to serve with Mark in student ministry. I've witnessed a tentative "yes" when he was first asked to serve, grow into a deep desire to see students enter into a lasting and thriving relationship with Jesus Christ. This book is evidence of his passion to see people develop as followers of Jesus. What a simple yet effective way to grow spiritually...15 minutes with Jesus.

†Cory Phillips, Youth Pastor, Madison United Methodist

FOREWORD

Jesus calls us to remain in him, to live with him, to abide with him. Being a Christian is not about a right belief. It is about a right relationship. That should come as no surprise because we are created in the image of a relational God, known to us in a beautiful connection as Father, Son, and Holy Spirit. And miracle of miracles, that God wants to be in relationship with us. Developing any healthy relationship takes time, especially when it is with the Lord of the Universe. That is what this book is about. Spending time with Jesus.

Mark Hikes writes from personal experience and I have been blessed to share in his story as a pastor and a brother in Jesus. He is a Christ-follower who deeply desires to bring others along on the journey. Mark is an influencer, not in a pop culture or social media manner but in a very Christ-like way. He draws people together, youth and adults alike, and in the process we find ourselves being drawn closer to God. His own transformation gives credence to the truth which he shares in this volume.

The author has learned that the key to developing a relationship with Jesus is sharing life with him. He invites us to do the same. *15 Minutes with Jesus* is not a methodology about developing small groups. It does not offer a checklist of steps for powerful disciple making. Different from another bible study, it is an example, a witness if you will, to one way in which lives can be transformed by the power of the Holy Scripture as it is applied to everyday life.

If you are seeking a deeper relationship with Christ, on a personal level, or within your shared life with others, I encourage you to spend some time with this book. More importantly, spend 15 minutes with Jesus. You will forever be glad that you did.

Rev. Jim Genesse
Starkville, Mississippi

REMAIN IN ME, AS I ALSO REMAIN IN YOU.
JOHN 15:4 NIV

PREFACE

Here's the deal... I believe that we simply do not spend enough time with Jesus. How much time is enough? I'm not really sure. You may pray every day. You may read the Bible every day. You may read some other Christian book every day. You may do all three. You may not do any of it.

One thing I am sure of is that spending consistent time with Jesus every day is the most important part of a Christian journey. It doesn't matter if you are a new Christian, mature Christian or someone who has not accepted Jesus as your Lord and Savior yet. He wants to spend time with you. He wants to be close to you.

I have the great privilege of being one of three family group leaders for an incredible group of 10th graders at my church. They are very important to me. I love them and love the journey we are on together. Early on, in one of our discussions, we talked about how much time is enough.

Here is my take, quality is more important than quantity. The next thing is being consistent with your time. So, my personal belief is that if you can spend 15 minutes a day with Him, that would be a great start. All of us can carve out 15 minutes. In fact, I'm guessing that finding 15 minutes would be pretty easy. But guess what? I'm pretty sure that Jesus would love and appreciate 15 minutes of your time. My students have heard that phrase hundreds of times. That is why the title makes so much sense!

Why is the book written in text boxes? I'm glad you asked. Text messages are where the heart of the book started. When the quarantine began in March of 2020, we were not able to gather in person to worship together. Sure, we immediately started meeting on zoom calls, but it just didn't seem like it was enough.

I was definitely missing the group, after just two or three weeks, and we really had no idea when we would be back to in person worship. I wanted to do more to stay connected, with them. So, I decided to start sending a daily text. The first week was simply some of my favorite Bible verses. The group seemed to like the idea. So, I wanted to make it better. After that first week I made the decision to make a weekly theme, that way I could share different verses from all over the Bible about one topic. The feedback I received from the students was really cool, so the text is still going today.

Did you notice the paracord fish on the cover? This rope was part of my favorite message I have ever done with the group. This particular piece of rope is braided with several different strands but still has an inner core that helps keep the strands together. It represents our relationship with Jesus. Each one of us represents a different strand of the rope. The center represents Jesus. We are woven together as one group, as a family. We are all significant to one another. But as strong as we are, as a group, we still have to keep Jesus at the center of our lives.

Jesus must be at the center of everything we do!! The color of the rope is important too. This rope is highly visible. Is your relationship with Jesus highly visible? Can people see that you follow Jesus by your actions and your words? Jesus is like the best friend we could ever have! Let's tell everyone about Him!

So, why don't you join us? Start your 15 minutes with Jesus every day by reading this book. Use it and refer back to your Bible to look at the scripture that comes before and after each day's reading. Make notes using the free space on the pages in this book. What did a particular day make you think about? How did it make you feel? I hope you enjoy reading it as much as I enjoyed writing it. This has been an AMAZING journey! I would love to hear from you... what you like about this book, what you would like to see in a future book, or just to talk about your journey. Call or email me: (717) 439-8575 or mhhikes@gmail.com.

Mark Hikes, Author

...with his give...
...ut him were sp...
...me to arrest him.

for only a short time now;
...ne one who sent me.
...d will not find me:»

...other, 'Where is he going...
...road to the people who a...
...reeks? •What does he mean...
and will not find me:

...day of the festival,° Jesus st...

...let him come to me!ᴾ
...d drink •who believes in m...
...ast �q shall flow fountains of li...ng water.ʳ
...which those who believed in him were to receive...
...because Jesus had not yet been glorified.

...of the Messiah

...n listening said, 'Surely he must be the prophet'...
...rist', but others said, 'Would the Christ be from...
...ay that the Christ must be descended from David...
...ethlehem?'ᵗ •So the people could not agree about...
...to arrest him, but no one actually laid hands on...

...he chief priests and Pharisees who said to them...
...im?' •The police replied, 'There has never been...
...him'. •So' the Pharisees answered 'you have been...
...ny of the authorities believed in him? Any of the...
...ows nothing about the Law—they are damned...
...he same man who had come to Jesus earlier—said to...
...oes not allow us to pass judgement on a man without...
...covering what he is about?' •To this they answered...
...o into the matter, and see for yourself: prophets do...

14
...d Jesus went to the Mount of Olives.
...in the Temple again; and as all the people...
...each them.

Heart

THE MORE WE FILL OUR HEARTS WITH JESUS,
THE LESS ROOM WE HAVE FOR SIN.
OUR HEARTS WILL BE KEPT BY THE WORD,
IF WE KEEP THE WORD IN OUR HEARTS!

Did you ever notice that EVERY time you go to the doctor, he or she listens to your heart? You know why that is? It's because the heart is one of our body's most important organs. It's like the engine for our body. The doctor wants to make sure it's healthy.

Well, our heart, is also critical in our relationship with Jesus!

So.... what if Jesus put that stethoscope on your heart, to check your spiritual health? What would He find?

In today's verse, Ezekiel is writing to the Israelites living in exile. Early on, Ezekiel warned them that their worship of false gods would be judged. Later, after Jerusalem's destruction, he wrote to encourage them, making sure they understood God would bring them back. God promised not only to bring the people back, but also to completely change their hearts.

I WILL GIVE YOU A NEW HEART AND PUT A NEW SPIRIT IN YOU; I WILL REMOVE FROM YOU YOUR HEART OF STONE AND GIVE YOU A HEART OF FLESH.
EZEKIEL 36:26

How about that heart transplant? 😊 🖤 Figurative language of course.... Their hearts were cold and unfeeling. They were angry people. Things weren't going "their way". They were unable to respond to God's love.

God transformed them. He gave them hearts of flesh. Hearts that were spiritually alive and open to Him. So you see, as Christians, we get to go through transformation. We get to have our hearts changed! Our new heart gives us new life. A new ability to LOVE like never before.

WHAT DID TODAY MAKE ME THINK ABOUT?
IS MY HEART OPEN TO JESUS?

I SEEK YOU WITH ALL MY HEART;
DO NOT LET ME STRAY FROM YOUR COMMANDS.
I HAVE HIDDEN YOUR WORD IN MY HEART THAT
I MIGHT NOT SIN AGAINST YOU.
PSALM 119: 10-11

"Hidden your word in my heart"? How can we hide God's word in our heart? Well, we can study God's word. We can share The Word with others. We can pray for strength to help us obey His commands.

As we study His Word, it helps us gain understanding. Then, as we gain understanding and really get to know God's word, eventually it becomes part of who we are. Studying the word and sharing the word becomes a daily part of our lives. It becomes the first thing we do every day because of our excitement of growing closer to Him. Soon, we start to think and behave differently, because we have filled our hearts with Jesus!

The more we fill our hearts with Jesus, the less room we have for sin. So, the conclusion on today's verses;

Our hearts will be kept by The Word, if we keep The Word in our hearts!

Read more, spend more time, share more, ask more questions about Jesus. Let's get our hearts so filled up with Jesus, that there isn't room for doubt or sin.

HOW CAN I SPEND MORE TIME IN THE WORD?
HOW MUCH ROOM IS IN MY HEART FOR JESUS?

Do we have submissive hearts? If you think about it, for us to receive and understand, Jesus commands we have a submissive heart.

THE WISE IN HEART ACCEPT COMMANDS,
BUT A CHATTERING FOOL COMES TO RUIN.
PROVERBS 10:8

It isn't just about listening to Jesus. We receive instructions from others in our life, too. Who else do we receive input from?

- Parents
- Teachers
- Pastors
- Mentors
- Coaches

Think about situations where those people in our lives give us commands or instructions. We need to have submissive hearts in those situations also. A submissive heart makes us wise.

So you see, it all goes together! When we open our hearts, when we submit to receiving instruction and commands from others in our life, we learn A LOT. We may learn the difference between right and wrong or what's good for us and what isn't. Our decision to "listen" (submit) to others who influence our life helps shape who we are.

We gain wise hearts. Having a wise heart helps shape our lives. Are you open to receiving instructions/commands from others? And Jesus?

Are you wise in heart?

DO I HAVE A SUBMISSIVE HEART?
AM I OPEN TO RECEIVING INSTRUCTIONS?

God wants our whole heart, not just part of it. Joel reminded us of that when he wrote to the people of Judah. At the time, Judah was going through a change in leadership. Idol worship was flourishing. Joel wrote to warn them that judgment would come if they didn't repent. He was sure it was the time for people to change their ways. He was urging them to return to God.

"EVEN NOW," DECLARES THE LORD, "RETURN TO ME WITH ALL YOUR HEART, WITH FASTING AND WEEPING AND MOURNING."
JOEL 2:12

The people received their warning. Because of the coming judgment, God's people should repent. Do you think their repentance will be accepted, if they are scared into it? Is their repentance less valid?

I don't think so. God simply wants to be in relationship with us. The important thing is that they return to God with sincerity. Just as for us today, we have to go to God with all our heart and surrender to Him.

HAVE I STARTED TO GIVE MY HEART TO JESUS? HOW DOES THAT MAKE ME FEEL?

I talk a lot about spending 15 minutes a day with Jesus. I truly hope you realize how insignificant that amount of time is to you, but how important it would be to Jesus!

In today's verse the psalmist is asking God for help in evaluating the use of his time. He's praying for wisdom to understand the shortness of life.

TEACH US TO NUMBER OUR DAYS, THAT WE MAY GAIN A HEART OF WISDOM.
PSALM 90:12

There are many things in our life that we can count on, so many "sure things." However, the length of our lifetime is not one of them. Tomorrow is never promised.

Pause and reflect on how you use your time. This verse tells me to treasure every moment and do good in that moment. Use our time wisely for the Lord. Maximize the time we have to learn about Jesus, and share Him with others.

Now... we can all look back and see where we've wasted time on foolish things. We can't get that time back, but we can focus on what's in front of us. Time is like money, we can spend it wisely or foolishly, but it can never be spent again.

"Teach us" implies we have something to learn. Through prayer, I want God to open our hearts, even more, so we gain a heart of wisdom, to maximize the time we have to make Him most important.

Good things become bad things when they keep us from the best thing.

CAN I COMMIT TO 15 MINUTES A DAY WITH JESUS?
WHAT WILL I STOP DOING TO MAKE TIME FOR HIM?

You can't judge a book by its cover. How concerned are you about how you look? How you dress? Is your outward appearance consuming you? We all go through stuff like this. It doesn't matter if you're 16 or 52. One thing you need to remember is God doesn't care! You know what He cares about? Let's see what He says to Samuel, as a new king was about to be chosen.

BUT THE LORD SAID TO SAMUEL "DO NOT CONSIDER HIS APPEARANCE OR HIS HEIGHT, FOR I HAVE REJECTED HIM. THE LORD DOES NOT LOOK AT THE THINGS PEOPLE LOOK AT. PEOPLE LOOK AT THE OUTWARD APPEARANCE, BUT THE LORD LOOKS AT THE HEART.
1 SAMUEL 16:7

Verses 1 through 13 give you the whole story. Samuel needed to be reminded that God's anointed were not chosen because of physical attributes. This was difficult for Samuel to understand. He was used to kings whose only positive attributes were their physical prowess! But God looks at the heart.

THE LIFE OF A MAN WILL REFLECT HIS HEART.
MATTHEW 12:34-35

Saul, who had been king, was a head taller than his competition, he was physically strong and was super handsome, but he had greatly disappointed the Lord. The Lord explains to Samuel, don't look at outward appearance. Someone may look strong but be the weakest when it comes to sin. The Lord was looking for someone who would love Him with ALL his heart!

HOW DID TODAY'S VERSE MAKE ME FEEL?
HOW AM I DOING WITH MY 15 MINUTES?

Here's the deal... it is important for us to understand that what's on the inside is way more important than our outside! I can tell you that over and over, and I know it's something we all hear growing up, and then we all give that advice to others, when we become adults. It is just that IMPORTANT to understand!

Live your life with a BIG HEART; for Jesus and for others. ♥

YOUR BEAUTY SHOULD NOT COME FROM OUTWARD ADORNMENT, SUCH AS ELABORATE HAIRSTYLES AND THE WEARING OF GOLD JEWELRY OR FINE CLOTHES. RATHER, IT SHOULD BE THAT OF YOUR INNER SELF, THE UNFADING BEAUTY OF A GENTLE AND QUIET SPIRIT, WHICH IS OF GREAT WORTH IN GOD'S SIGHT.
1 PETER 3:3-4

God doesn't care how much bling you have on the outside. He only cares how much bling you have on the inside! He only cares about your heart. Our true beauty should not be an outward beauty but the beauty of Christ within us.

Being a Christian, is having a brand new heart. A heart that is not only filled with Jesus, but focused on helping others fill their hearts, too.

WHAT IS THE MOST IMPORTANT THING I CAN SHARE WITH SOMEONE ELSE ABOUT THIS WEEK?

Reliability

WHAT IF WE ALL MADE A PROMISE TO GOD?
WHAT IF WE PROMISED TO
SPEND TIME WITH HIM EVERY DAY?
WHAT IF WE PROMISED TO SPEND TIME
WITH HIM FOR THE REST OF OUR LIVES?

When you think of God, do you ever think about how reliable He is? We honestly don't give it enough thought, do we? Could we possibly even be taking Him for granted? I'd like to spend this week looking at God's reliability in our lives.

KNOW THEREFORE THAT THE LORD, YOUR GOD, IS GOD; HE IS THE FAITHFUL GOD, KEEPING HIS COVENANT OF LOVE TO A THOUSAND GENERATIONS OF THOSE WHO LOVE HIM AND KEEP HIS COMMANDMENTS.

DEUTERONOMY 7:9

List things that are constant in our lives: health, shelter, freedom to choose, people who love us. Just to name a few. Now think about how easy it is to take things like that for granted. What do we have in our lives that is more constant than God? Nothing I can think of.

God promised His covenant of love to a thousand generations!

- Exodus 20:6
- Deuteronomy 1:11

Let's say a generation is 50 years. That's 50,000 years! I would say that is pretty reliable. What if we all made a promise to God? What if we promised to spend time with him every day? What if we promised to spend time with him for the rest of our lives?

Rather than taking him for granted, let's take advantage of the fact that He is there for us every minute of every day. Let's learn from Him. Let's walk with him. Let's talk to Him... every day. Let's show God how reliable we can be! 💜🙏

DO I TAKE JESUS FOR GRANTED?
WHAT THINGS IN MY LIFE AM I THANKFUL FOR?

How reliable are we? How honest are we with ourselves? With God? I really want you to understand this whole reliability thing is a two way street. We should be reliable to God. He should be able to count on the fact that we will to spend time with Him every day!

THE LORD IS NEAR TO ALL WHO CALL ON HIM, TO ALL WHO CALL ON HIM IN TRUTH.
PSALM 145:18

We cannot trick God! When we worship, when we talk to Him, it must be done with sincerity. It CAN NOT be lip service. We must worship Him with our hearts.

It's special to know how close He is to us. We know he's there, because He's so reliable. Because God is so reliable, He deserves our best.

God will always hear us. Are we talking to Him with a sincere approach of strengthening our relationship with Him? He hears what we say AND sees our heart! God will not be fooled. He will respond to us as we are, not as we profess to be. He knows us. He knows the truth.

HOW RELIABLE AM I IN MY RELATIONSHIP WITH JESUS? WHAT AM I DOING TO SPEND TIME WITH HIM?

> GIVE THANKS TO THE LORD, FOR HE IS
> GOOD, HIS LOVE ENDURES FOREVER.
> **PSALM 107:1**

We see God's reliability over and over. How He forgives His people and shows mercy on them. Time after time, they continue to make poor choices. Time after time He rescues them. Not sometimes, EVERY time. **God will NEVER let us down.** No matter how close we get to Him, it is still hard to understand how much He LOVES us!

> LET THEM GIVE THANKS TO THE LORD FOR HIS
> UNFAILING LOVE AND HIS WONDERFUL DEEDS
> FOR MANKIND, FOR HE SATISFIES THE THIRSTY
> AND FILLS THE HUNGRY WITH GOOD THINGS.
> **PSALM 107:8-9**

Today's verse made me think of that list from a few days ago, about things we take for granted. We don't think much about food or water, as it relates to our physical life.

Because God is so reliable, we don't have to worry about hunger or thirst in our spiritual life either, yet sometimes we let our relationship reach dangerous levels of dehydration. We have a willing teacher who wants us to come to eat and drink with Him. **There is no reason to be thirsty.**

It's odd to think how long 2,000 to 3,000 years ago really is. That would be about 50 generations, right? Obviously, a lot has changed! But one thing remains the same. God is as reliable today as He was then.

WHAT WAYS CAN I SEE GOD'S RELIABILITY?
HOW CAN I SHOW MY RELIABILITY TO JESUS?

Wouldn't it be reassuring to know the good things in our lives would stay constant? You know... we have that in Jesus.

REMEMBER YOUR LEADERS, WHO SPOKE THE WORD OF GOD TO YOU. CONSIDER THE OUTCOME OF THEIR WAY OF LIFE AND IMITATE THEIR FAITH. JESUS CHRIST IS THE SAME YESTERDAY AND TODAY, AND FOREVER.
HEBREWS 13:7-8

If you don't have Jesus in your life, I want you to know, He's there waiting for you. If we do have a relationship with Jesus, we need to work continuously to strengthen our bond with Him. He should be a constant part of our lives.

Most likely, there is someone in our life that led us to Jesus. Think about how much that person cares about you. They loved you so much, they shared Jesus with you. That's a very powerful bond which should never be forgotten. But, Jesus should be #1. Jesus needs to be the center of our heart.

Verse 8 shows reliability for sure. Jesus is the same today as He was in the beginning. There are so many examples throughout the Bible that show us.

In Malachi 3:6, He tells us He does not change. Revelation 1:17 says "I am the First and the Last." Jesus is there for us, just as He is for everyone. He was, He is, and He is always going to be! That constant presence should be reassuring for us all.

FOR ME TO MAKE JESUS PART OF EVERY DAY, I NEED TO...?
WHAT IS MY RELIABILITY ON A SCALE OF 1-10?

Have you seen those yard signs that say, this house is protected by _____ security? I'm guessing the sign serves two purposes. It is a deterrent for potential intruders, while it is also serving as an advertisement for the security company. As Christians, we have pretty reliable security. God guards our eternal safety! What could be more reliable than that?

LET THOSE WHO LOVE THE LORD HATE EVIL, FOR HE GUARDS THE LIVES OF HIS FAITHFUL ONES AND DELIVERS THEM FROM THE HAND OF THE WICKED.
PSALM 97:10

This verse is NOT saying we will live a life free of adversity. There are times He allows adversity in our lives. Those times are part of our lives because there are greater things planned for us. He is looking at a BIGGER picture that we can't even begin to understand. God is most concerned with our eternal safety.

His grace should inspire us to live better lives and do our best to be Christ-like. We learn the difference between good and evil, because He teaches us. We are all accepted by God if we love Him. But, understand that loving Him is being in constant relationship with Him. He wants us to be reliable in our worship.

We should get signs for our front yards that say "this house and the people in it are protected by Jesus"! Who's with me?

AM I GIVING MY BEST TO JESUS RIGHT NOW? HOW?

Reliability can help bring us comfort. Knowing that certain things in our lives are going to remain the same is good. It gives us reassurance. Take a minute and think about the things on that list....
Did you include God?

~~~~~~

THE GRASS WITHERS AND THE FLOWERS FALL,
BUT THE WORD OF GOD ENDURES FOREVER.
ISAIAH 40:8

~~~~~~

This verse makes me feel good. I feel reassured and have a feeling of hope. I love seasons, and Spring is the beginning of so much. Grass starts to grow, trees get their leaves, and shrubs begin to flower. It's like spring starts the cycle.

There is no cycle with God. He's with us every minute, of every day. He never leaves us. He's not hot or cold.

Everything in creation can go through phases. Everything has a season. Everything will wither. That is one of the reasons having God as our foundation is so important. We know He is going to be there for us... every day.

We can go to Him first thing in the morning, or we can go to Him late at night. It doesn't matter what time it is or what we need to bring him. He's there!

#RELIABLEFRIEND

WHAT ARE THE CONSTANT THINGS IN MY LIFE?
IS JESUS ONE OF THEM?

God is good, all the time! And all the time, God is good! And forever! You and I know that, but we need to make sure everyone else does.

YOU, LORD, ARE FORGIVING AND GOOD, ABOUNDING IN LOVE TO ALL WHO CALL ON YOU. HEAR MY PRAYER, LORD; LISTEN TO MY CRY FOR MERCY. WHEN I AM IN DISTRESS, I CALL TO YOU, BECAUSE YOU ANSWER ME.
PSALM 86:5-7

Not only is God reliable with His presence, but everything in our lives comes from God. **He is generous with His love and everything He gives us.** And it shows for hundreds of years.

Just look at the history of how reliable He is. How many times did He forgive the Israelites on their journey through the wilderness to the promised land. We have wilderness in our lives today, right? We wander, right? We all go through periods in our lives where we are just not sure... where we have doubt. All of this is happening to us, on the journey to our own promised land. Our journey to heaven!

We need to trust God in our prayers during those times, understanding He is in control and we receive the same forgiveness today the Israelites did more than 2,000 years ago. The reliability I feel from God helps me know He loves me and there's hope for all of us who call on Him.

CAN JESUS COUNT ON ME TO SHARE HIS WORD? WHAT WERE MY BIGGEST TAKEAWAYS FROM THIS WEEK?

Love

ARE WE SHARING GOD'S WORD
AND HIS LOVE? ARE WE TAKING TIME
TO ENSURE OTHER PEOPLE UNDERSTAND
HOW MUCH HE LOVES THEM?
TRUE LOVE IS MORE THAN A FEELING, IT
IS A CONSISTENT ATTITUDE OF GIVING
OURSELVES TO GOD AND TO OTHERS.

Let's kick off our section about love with a beautiful verse that has a really simple but powerful three-word sentence right in the middle.

AND SO WE KNOW AND RELY ON THE LOVE GOD HAS FOR US. GOD IS LOVE. WHOEVER LIVES IN LOVE LIVES IN GOD, AND GOD IN THEM.

1 JOHN 4:16

This gives me such a peaceful feeling! Read it again...just that middle sentence... Amazing. He is always with us. Our friends may come and go, the importance of other people in our lives will change over the years, but we know God loves us, no matter what.

We never need to feel lonely, because we have God filling us. His love is not temporary or occasional.

His love is FOREVER!!

If we are truly filled with God's love it should show in how we interact with others. Are we sharing His word and His love? Are we taking time to ensure other people understand how much He loves them?

True love is more than a feeling, it is a consistent attitude of giving ourselves to God and to others!

How can we show that? How can we GIVE that today?

HOW CAN I SHOW GOD'S LOVE THIS WEEK?
HOW COMFORTABLE DO I FEEL SHARING GOD'S LOVE?

Love is a very powerful emotion! To tell someone you love them should really mean something. Can we say that we love God, if we don't obey him? Not really? Let's look at what John has to say:

WHOEVER HAS MY COMMANDS AND KEEPS THEM IS THE ONE WHO LOVES ME. THE ONE WHO LOVES ME WILL BE LOVED BY MY FATHER, AND I TOO WILL LOVE THEM AND SHOW MYSELF TO THEM.
JOHN 14:21

Well that keeps it pretty clear. This is one of those times where our talks about 15 minutes a day in the Bible comes in handy.

So, as we can see, love for Christ and obedience is inseparable.

Here we see why it is important to be in God's word, and learn God's word. If we are learning His word, we will learn His will. It is so important for us to know God's will, so we can do His will.

IF YOU LOVE ME, KEEP MY COMMANDS.
JOHN 14:15

CAN WE SAY WE LOVE GOD IF WE DON'T OBEY HIM? HOW ARE LOVE AND OBEYING THE SAME?

Read John 15-21. It is an AMAZING passage about His love for us and what our love for Him should look like. He is promising the Holy Spirit to us. He's making sure we understand that we are never alone.

If you say it, you better mean it!

LOVE MUST BE SINCERE. HATE WHAT IS EVIL;
CLING TO WHAT IS GOOD.
ROMANS 12:9

Our love should be pure and sincere. It should be shared/shown without being self-centered and definitely without any behind the scenes motives.

We need to love faithfully and care for others, despite the response we receive. Through our relationship with Jesus, we learn how to love. And that includes loving people who may not love us, or share our beliefs.

One more verse for today...

YOU HAVE LOVED RIGHTEOUSNESS AND
HATED WICKEDNESS; THEREFORE GOD, YOUR
GOD, HAS SET YOU ABOVE YOUR COMPANIONS
BY ANOINTING YOU WITH THE OIL OF JOY.
HEBREWS 1:9

It is important to God for us to love our brothers and sisters in Christ and to love Him.

Love is a POWERFUL emotion!

IS IT HARD FOR ME TO LOVE EVERYONE?
HOW CAN I TRULY LOVE EVERYONE?

♡ ♡ ♡

Are you ALL IN? Sometimes our love can be tested, even our love for God.

Jesus makes it very clear here... Loving God is the most important command to keep.

LOVE THE LORD YOUR GOD WITH ALL YOUR HEART AND WITH ALL YOUR SOUL AND WITH ALL YOUR MIND AND WITH ALL YOUR STRENGTH.

MARK 12:30

The word ALL is used in each of these commands. It doesn't say half of, or quarter of, or 90% of. It says ALL!!

Jesus left NO doubt at all about what position the Lord your God must have in our lives. Above all, He must be Lord. He must be the most important thing in our lives.

He mentions the heart first because it is the CENTER of our being. We are what our heart is. Our will is involved with the soul. Our heart really is at the center of who we are and what actions we take! We need to make sure we are ALL IN—ALL THE TIME!!

WHAT DOES JESUS TELL US ABOUT LOVING OTHERS? AM I PREPARED TO FOLLOW THE EXAMPLES JESUS SET FOR ME?

"Man, my neighbor... 😡 that guy is such a... 🤬."

We must be careful slinging around those nasty words toward our neighbors. Jesus is pretty clear in today's verse that after loving Him with all our heart, the second most important person on the list is... YEP! You guessed it. 😊

THE SECOND IS THIS:
LOVE YOUR NEIGHBOR AS YOURSELF.
THERE IS NO COMMANDMENT GREATER THAN THESE.
MARK 12:31

"Love God with ALL your heart. Love your neighbor as yourself." Then Jesus says, "there is no commandment greater than these." If you think about it, the other commandments really get helped if we get these two right. Have a great day.

CAN OTHERS SEE MY LOVE FOR JESUS?
HOW IS MY 15 MINUTES A DAY GOING?

Is our love for others optional?
Let's see what Jesus says about that.

~~~~~~~~~~~~~~~~~~~~~~~~~~~~~~~~

MY COMMAND IS THIS:
LOVE EACH OTHER AS I HAVE LOVED YOU.
JOHN 15:12

~~~~~~~~~~~~~~~~~~~~~~~~~~~~~~~~

You can quickly see, it is NOT optional for us to love others. This is a commandment of the Lord. Love for other people is a true test of genuine fellowship. Honestly, this can be very difficult for us, no matter where we are at on our journey as Christians. We will be tested.

You've heard me talk about it before. Do we have the ability to love everyone, including people who may not love us. Jesus showed us how to do that. He set an example for us.

Are we prepared to follow?

DO I HAVE JESUS AT THE CENTER OF MY LIFE? AM I ALL IN?

Jesus talked to the disciples and gave them a "new" command.

A NEW COMMAND I GIVE YOU; LOVE ONE ANOTHER. AS I HAVE LOVED YOU, SO YOU MUST LOVE ONE ANOTHER. BY THIS EVERYONE WILL KNOW THAT YOU ARE MY DISCIPLES, IF YOU LOVE ONE ANOTHER.
JOHN 13:34-35

He knew some of them had been jealous of each another. The disciples were from different backgrounds, and he thought they might have trouble working together. To stop all of this Jesus gave them a new commandment. Not a suggestion... a commandment.

He did not stop with "love one another", either. He added, "as I have loved you". This means to have unselfish love. Jesus loves us not because of things we do, but in spite of them.

Jesus is saying that this great, unselfish love will set them apart from the rest of the world, because not everyone can love like this. Love unselfishly today!

HOW DID THIS WEEK MAKE ME FEEL? 🖤
HOW CAN I SHOW LOVE TO MY NEIGHBOR?

Prayer

PRAYER IS LIKE THE LUNGS OF A HEALTHY
RELATIONSHIP WITH THE FATHER.
PRAYER IS OUR DAILY CONTACT WITH HIM.
IT KEEPS US ACTIVE.
IT KEEPS OUR RELATIONSHIP HEALTHY.
IT IS HOW WE GET HELP AND STRENGTH.
AND A WAY FOR US TO PRAISE.

There was a time I struggled in my prayer life. I think there are times in all of our lives that we have these questions...

- How do I pray?
- Where do I pray?
- What should I pray for?

I'm sure in your head you just added more questions to this list. Let's look at it like this. Instead of trying to figure out what prayer is, let's talk about, what prayer is not.

God wants us ALL to pray, right? It doesn't matter if you are 5 years old, 15, 55, or 105? I don't think He meant for prayer to be professor-like, because He wants all of us to be able to communicate with Him.

Prayer is not a formula. For example, you don't pray a certain prayer in a certain way that God will be more likely to give you what you ask for. Prayer is not a way for us to try to get God to bend to our will.

Prayer is not something that we should do just because we're supposed to or because we think it will get us on His good side.

So, what is prayer? Prayer is a conversation between us and God.

It is an ongoing conversation during which we get to know Him more intimately. I often think about it as talking to the BEST OF THE BEST FRIEND EVER!

God certainly has the qualities we would want in a best friend...

- He listens to us.
- He is honest.
- He will always be by our side.
- He loves us unconditionally.
- He will ALWAYS accept us.

HOW IMPORTANT IS IT TO PRAY?
WHAT DOES PRAYER MEAN TO ME?

You're not listening to me!!
Could I have your attention, please??

IN THE MORNING, LORD, YOU HEAR MY VOICE; IN THE MORNING I LAY MY REQUESTS BEFORE YOU AND WAIT EXPECTANTLY.
PSALM 5:3

Jesus hears your voice every time you pray to Him. You don't have to yell! You don't have to wake Him up. You don't have to grab His attention, because you already have it.

When you take time out of your day to talk to Him, *Jesus will put everything else down to listen to you.*

He never has too much going on, and never interrupts you, mid-sentence. Jesus will simply listen, because he wants to hear exactly what you have to say. He is always there with an open ear.

WHEN IS MY FAVORITE TIME TO PRAY? HOW MUCH TIME DO I SET ASIDE FOR PRAYER?

When do I pray? When should I pray?

For starters, Paul gives us a short, little reminder:

PRAY CONTINUALLY.
1 THESSALONIANS 5:17

That's it. Short, sweet, and to the point. Pray ALL the time. Jesus began his prayer in Matthew 6:9 by saying "Our Father". That is a reminder that prayer is more personal than ritual or mandatory. It is a conversation between God and ANYONE who has a relationship with Him. **We are welcome to come to God ANYTIME!!**

Get your Bible out, there's lots of examples!

- Jesus prayed early in the morning (Mark 1:35)...
- ... and in the evening (Mark 14:32)
- We can pray, when we are afraid (Palms 119:145-146)
- When we are in need (Matthew 7:7-12)
- When we lack wisdom (James 1:5)
- We can pray to express our joy (Philippians 1:5)
- ...and gratitude we feel, when we see God at work around us (1 Thessalonians 5:16-18)

Although very important to Christian health, prayer is not meant to be scientific, difficult, or extravagant. Prayer is simply a heart-filled conversation between us and God.

WHAT DOES "PRAY CONTINUALLY" MEAN TO ME? MY FAVORITE EXAMPLE OF PRAYER IS...

Where do I pray? Where should I pray?

So, now we know we can pray any time. Well guess what? Those prayers can also be offered in any place.

In 1 Samuel 1:9-11, Hannah prayed to the Lord in the temple to give her a son. That prayer was no more spiritual than Moses' prayer in the desert where he prayed to God for forgiveness after the golden calf incident in Exodus 32:11-14.

Let's look at a few more examples:

- Jesus prayed in a garden (Mark 14:32-42)
- Paul prayed in prison (Acts 16:22-25)
- Nehemiah prayed in the king's court (Nehemiah 2:4)
- Jonah even prayed in the belly of a fish (Jonah 2:1-10)

I talk to Jesus A LOT in my truck! No matter where we are, when we pray we can ALWAYS be assured of great reception with God.

WHERE DO I FEEL MOST COMFORTABLE PRAYING?
HOW AM I DOING WITH MY 15 MINUTES?

Why should we pray?

So in the verse below, it's really important to know what is going on. Look at Acts 6:1-3. This group of leaders is like, we need to take care of this so that we can focus on prayer.

...BUT WE WILL GIVE OURSELVES CONTINUALLY TO PRAYER AND TO THE MINISTRY OF THE WORD.
ACTS 6:4

Hmmm...

Prayer and then to the ministry of the word. Our healthy prayer life gives us power to be able to carry out the ministry of the word.

I was reading a bible study this week that gave me a cool prayer perspective..... Prayer has the effect that we move God's hands. If we pray for someone in Australia, God's hands move over to Australia, and He works on those who we are interceding for. Looking at it that way, prayer gives us an extended reach all over the world. 😊🖤

Do you need another Why??? Because we can use our prayer power to help other people. Prayer is an incredible, amazing ministry.

WHY SHOULD I MAKE PRAYER IMPORTANT?
WHO CAN I PRAY FOR TODAY?

How many times in a day do you think about breathing? Prayer should be like breathing.

- We know why we should.
- We know that it doesn't matter where or when.
- So, what are people waiting for? 😊

We can only live a few minutes without breathing, right? My aunt suffered with a breathing illness. If she talked more than about 10 minutes, she would get sharp pains in her side. A breathing condition can affect your entire body.

Prayer is like the lungs of a healthy relationship with the Father. Prayer is our daily contact with Him. It keeps us active. It keeps our relationship healthy. It is how we get help and strength. And prayer is a way for us to praise Him.

Breathing goes almost unnoticed in our daily lives, yet it is critical for our survival.

What about prayer?

IS MY PRAYER TIME INTENTIONAL?
AM I PRAYING WITH A PURPOSE?
DO I TRY TO KEEP THINGS FROM GOD?

How familiar does this sound? *Dad knows you did it. Mom already knows what happened*. You won't understand until some day when you're a parent yourself. Maybe it's a gift we get with parenthood. 😏

There are no secrets. It is not classified information! HE ALREADY KNOWS.

DO NOT BE LIKE THEM, FOR YOUR FATHER KNOWS WHAT YOU NEED, BEFORE YOU ASK HIM.
MATTHEW 6:8

ASK AND IT WILL BE GIVEN TO YOU; SEEK AND YOU WILL FIND; KNOCK AND THE DOOR WILL BE OPENED FOR YOU.
MATTHEW 7:7

God wants you to humble yourself and ask Him. He wants you to ask Him for your needs. This is another great example of the "why" part. Reading the Bible is important. Talking to other people about Jesus is important. Church and youth groups are important.

Prayer is YOUR conversation with God! It is your time to talk to him. When we are praying, we are not studying Him; we are with Him.

WHAT IS MY BIGGEST TAKE AWAY FROM THIS WEEK? HOW WAS MY 15 MINUTES A DAY THIS WEEK?

MARK'S TESTIMONY

Prayer is a huge part of our personal journey with Jesus, but I didn't always think that way.

If you had asked me 20 years ago if I believed in God, my answer would have been, "Sure... doesn't everybody believe in God?" I realized, in 2013, that believing in God and understanding that Jesus is our Lord and Savior are two very different things. Someone could have helped me understand that Jesus is our Lord and Savior, but maybe never have gotten to the most important part about Jesus... Knowing He wants a relationship with me. That's the part that I just didn't know about until late 2012, early 2013.

Growing up, church was confusing. My mom and dad were both divorced when they met. My mother was raised Catholic and my father was Protestant. So, although Mom wanted to raise me in the Catholic Church, she lost that argument with Dad.

I remember two very important things about my church life growing up. First, I remember going to church EVERY Sunday. I'm sure I set attendance records for the average 8-year-old. The other thing I remember is that church was never part of anything else around me. We went to church every Sunday yet never talked about God any other time. I just figured that's what everyone did. I believe it was important for Dad to take me to church every week because that was what he was supposed to do.

Once I left home for college, the attendance streak was over. I started a new streak. One I'm not proud of, but I'm not afraid to talk about it, either. I didn't go to church for years. In fact, I didn't go to church at all, really, until I met my wife, Natalie. After asking her to marry me, I was a little nervous. We were engaged but didn't have a church home. Lucky for us, Natalie had it covered. She had a church in mind. She had gone there a few times and really liked the pastor.

There you go, we had it all figured out. We were married in 2002 and began attending church on a regular basis. Our first church got us through our wedding and DJ's baptism. Our attendance was OK, but certainly not what it needed to be. We had the perfect excuse. No one wanted to hear our kid crying during service. Our attendance had a lot of ups and downs. Once our pastor

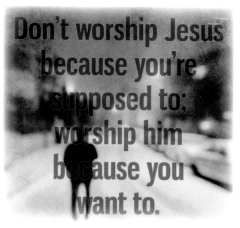

Don't worship Jesus because you're supposed to; worship him because you want to.

retired, we stopped going to church altogether. Isn't that the way it works? Your pastor retires and you retire with him?

We were in no hurry to find a new church until Jack was born. Natalie took control of the situation, and said, "Look, we have got to find a new church." We did eventually find one. Jack was baptized. It was all good. We were doing everything we were supposed to do as parents. We were checking all the boxes.

Honestly, we did regularly attend church at that point. We would probably be going to that same church if we still lived there. We moved to Alabama in October of 2010 and did attend church a few times in our sixteen months there. We liked the pastor but just never really got settled in. In February 2012, we moved to Mississippi.

After being in Madison, Mississippi a few months, we tried several churches without much success. On a Saturday in November, some friends from our neighborhood were sitting around the fire pit with us and told us all about their church. They convinced us to give it a try. The very next day was our first day in our current church.

While going in, we tried to stay off the radar of the welcoming committee. Thankfully, we sat down undetected. Just your normal good ole church service. Until the scripture was read.

> Look to the Lord and his strength; seek his face always.
> —1 Chronicles 16:11

Once that scripture was read and the pastor started preaching, I had the weirdest feeling. I mean, it was like I was the only person in the congregation that day. It felt like the pastor was talking directly to me.

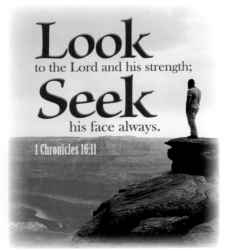

In fact, maybe he was. I remember getting in the car and asking Natalie, "Did you feel that?"

She certainly liked the sermon but did not know what I was taking about. We returned the next several Sundays and got involved in a small group which turned out to be very important for us.

We became members by Christmas. We had found a church home. Thank goodness, the search was over.

For the next few weeks after that first sermon from Pastor Jim, there were several other God instances that I saw and felt happening around me. The most important one involves the power of prayer.

When we first moved here, I heard it a lot.... "I'm praying for you brother." "Hey man, I'll say a prayer for you." I'll be honest, every time I heard someone say something of that nature, I would smile, and sometimes laugh, and think to myself, "who are you kidding, you ain't praying for them." I was actually cynical about it.

I was a Market Director for a big box retailer at the time. I love people and am genuinely interested in the lives of those who work with me. I would get to know things about their families, and they got to know all about mine.

A manager in one of the stores was walking the floor with me one day. As we were walking and talking, he remembered that our oldest son DJ was having some health concerns so he asked how things were going. I told him we had some tests coming up the next week that would give us a better idea what was going on. Though the issues were not too serious in nature, it was enough to keep these two parents worried.

When I told him about the tests, he said "I'd like to pray for you and your family." Kind of odd timing. I mean, you're standing in the middle of a retail store with your Market Director, telling him you're going to pray for him and his family. But, even though I may have thought it, I did not respond with my "sure you will" attitude. I was polite and said, "Thank you, I appreciate that."

But here's the catch... when he said, "I'd like to pray for you and your family," he meant RIGHT THERE. He reached out and grabbed my hand. NO WAY, this guy is not going to pray for me right now, in the middle of a store with customers EVERYWHERE! But, he did! He grabbed my hand and he prayed for me and my family.

That was odd to me, right? First, I finally witnessed someone carrying out their prayer commitment immediately. Then, the fact that he did it in the middle of an aisle with customers all around us. I mean, when we opened our eyes, there were customers waiting to ask us questions.

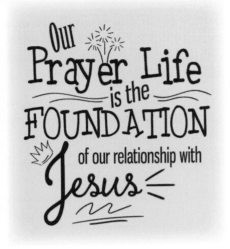
Our Prayer Life is the FOUNDATION of our relationship with Jesus

The last thing that really made me think... I never stopped him. I never made it awkward. I just thought to myself, this man is so committed to praying for my family, it would be a tragedy to stop him.

On the drive home, I felt thankful that Joe cared enough about me to pray for us, on the spot. He shared his faith with me in the most unlikely of places. That's what made it so special.

Several weeks later I was in one of my stores, and one of the managers came to my office. They had serious family issues going on. His wife was sick, and they were not quite sure what was going on. A series of tests were planned for the upcoming weeks. We talked about scheduling accommodations and other concerns about the business side of things. I wanted to make sure he kept me in the loop, and assured him his focus should be on his wife.

We talked a few more minutes. As we wrapped up the conversation, I said, "I'm going to pray for you and your family." I immediately thought to myself, "Wait, what? Where'd that come from?" It was almost like I said it out loud, because when I said I was going to pray for him and his family, he looked at me kind of odd.

He thanked me for my time and rose from his chair. At that moment, I got my command... "If you're going to pray for him, you pray for him right now." I was shocked at the voice I heard. It definitely got my attention. I asked if I could pray for him right now, and although he seemed a little uncomfortable, he allowed it. I moved closer, put my hand on his shoulder, and prayed. I can't even tell you what I said.

When we opened our eyes, he looked at me and asked, "Are you a Christian?" My response, "Ummmm I don't know. I'm not sure. Maybe? I guess so. Yes, yes actually, I am a Christian." He assured me that no one had ever prayed for him like that before.

When he left the office, I closed the door and sat there with my head in my hands for probably 15 minutes. Literally replaying the God things that had happened in the past few months.

After gathering myself, I picked up the phone and called Pastor Jim. I told him to clear his calendar; I was on my way to see him. We met in his office for hours. I accepted Jesus Christ as my Lord and Savior that day, and Jim was my witness.

Those months leading up to February 13, 2013, changed my life and my family's life forever! Much has happened in my relationship with Jesus since then, but it's a longer story. For now, I'll let you get back to YOUR 15 minutes with Jesus. Someday, however, I'll tell you the whole story... watch for it in another book coming soon. ☺

Strength

GOD IS FIRM.
GOD IS SOLID.
GOD IS IMMOVABLE.
GOD IS STABLE.

Paul was still concerned about the new believers in Thessalonica. He hoped to strengthen them with a stronger dose of advice than he gave them in his first letter.

> BUT THE LORD IS FAITHFUL, AND HE WILL STRENGTHEN YOU AND PROTECT YOU FROM THE EVIL ONE.
> **2 THESSALONIANS 3:3**

We get a lot of help from God against bad stuff, right? Get your bible out and read 1 Thessalonians verses 1 through 5.

Prayer, His love, and perseverance are all mentioned. And remember we also have the Armor. We know that we can rely on the Scriptures teachings and promises, just as Jesus did when he was under Satan's attacks.

I feel so much stronger in life being equipped with scripture, and knowing how much He loves me!!

HOW CAN GOD'S WORD GIVE ME STRENGTH?
HOW DID READING
2 THESSALONIANS 1-5 HELP ME?

This next verse comes from a chapter in my Bible titled "The Helper of Israel":

SO DO NOT FEAR, FOR I AM WITH YOU; DO NOT BE
DISMAYED, FOR I AM YOUR GOD.
I WILL STRENGTHEN YOU AND HELP YOU; I WILL
UPHOLD YOU WITH MY RIGHTEOUS RIGHT HAND.
ISAIAH 41:10

God is still comforting the Israelites after all they had done? God had called them to be His people from the time of Abraham to the time of their captivity.

His love for them was based on His own redeeming character and was not lessened by the sinful acts of his children. Whether it was judgment or comfort, He wanted the best for them.

God sees me mess up sometimes, but he still gives me strength! He just loves us so much!!

MY STRENGTH COMES FROM WHAT PART
OF MY RELATIONSHIP WITH JESUS?
GOD IS THE GREATEST SOURCE OF STRENGTH WE
HAVE. HOW DO WE SEE THAT IN OUR LIVES?

No Bible today. I want to share a personal story.

Yesterday, I'm driving along after picking up my sweet baby girl Emma from the vet. The news wasn't great. It had been a less than stellar day already. A real foot-stomping kind of day, if you know what I mean. I had a 30 minute drive, so I turned my Christian rock way up and rolled the windows down. And wouldn't you know it, every song that came on reminded me that Jesus is with me, even though I'm having a tough day.

So, here are my thoughts for you. When things are going our way, life is really easy isn't it? But at some point, all of us will encounter struggles and tough times.

Do you praise God when things are clicking? Have you ever "blamed" God, when you were struggling? You do understand that God is always the same, right? He never leaves us!

We have to remember that God is there with us when we are on top of the mountain, just like He's there for us when we fall down and are at the bottom of the mountain. When in one of those valleys, all we have to do is look up. He's there waiting for us to reach out and grab His hand, so He can pull us back up!

If you only ever remember one thing I've told you, make it this message!! 👊💪🖤

WHAT'S AN EXAMPLE OF HOW MY FAITH
HAS BEEN TESTED RECENTLY?
HOW CAN I BE SURE GOD IS ALWAYS WITH ME?

> I CAN DO ALL THINGS THROUGH HIM WHO
> GIVES ME STRENGTH.
> **PHILIPPIANS 4:13**

We've all heard this verse before. Paul was writing to the Philippians here to thank them for their monetary gifts. What does God give us strength to do, exactly?

He gives us strength to do everything He wants us to do. In Paul's life, it meant he had been given the ability to be content, whether he had plenty or if he was in great need. This is a verse that we can all relate to.

We just have to understand and believe that God's Grace will sustain us no matter where he leads us, even when we lack material things.

HOW DOES TODAY'S VERSE MAKE ME FEEL?
CAN WE HAVE STRENGTH
EVEN IF WE DON'T HAVE A LOT OF STUFF?

Remember the setting here. In this book, Paul is writing a letter to the "new guy". Timothy was facing all kinds of obstacles! False teachers and self-confidence were probably his two biggest challenges. So Paul is really trying to encourage him.

FOR THE SPIRIT GOD GAVE US DOES NOT MAKE US TIMID, BUT GIVES US POWER, LOVE, AND SELF DISCIPLINE.
2 TIMOTHY 1:7

Here's what I think about that verse. I think about a coach giving me a "pep" talk when I was younger, making sure I knew I was good enough. Making sure I knew he thought I was good enough.

The thing I want you to understand is whether it's a sporting event, school grades, dance competition, or whatever it is you do in LIFE, life is not a competition even if it may feel like that some days.

The Spirit God gives you does not make you timid but gives you power, love, and self discipline.

It's like we have super powers. 💪 Question is....

- Are you using them?
- How are you using them?
- Did you thank Him for them?
- How about 15 minutes today?

HAVE YOU EVER HAD TO STAND FIRM IN YOUR FAITH?
DO YOU THINK PAUL'S ADVICE WORKS TODAY?

From one of Paul's letters again this morning.

BE ON YOUR GUARD, STAND FIRM IN THE FAITH, BE COURAGEOUS, BE STRONG. DO EVERYTHING IN LOVE.
1 CORINTHIANS 16:13

I wish I could have met Paul. He just seems so down to earth, but also very serious. Again, this letter is to a new church in Corinth. Look at it like instructions to help them overcome obstacles they would encounter.

Well, guess what???

Read that verse 100 times. Apply to today? Sure does. Paul's advice is timeless!

HOW MUCH SELF-CONFIDENCE DOES JESUS GIVE ME?
HOW AM I USING MY SUPER POWERS?

Last day for strength!

A psalm of David:

TRULY MY SOUL FINDS REST IN GOD;
MY SALVATION COMES FROM HIM.
TRULY HE IS MY ROCK AND MY SALVATION;
HE IS MY FORTRESS, I WILL NEVER BE SHAKEN.
PSALM 62:1-2

God was the strong presence that an emotional guy like David needed.

In ancient times soldiers would look for large rocks and high ground to set up. It took fewer soldiers to defend. For us:

- God is firm.
- God is solid.
- God is immovable.
- God is stable.

How awesome is that? We get to be part of His family. That makes me feel safe! How about you?

WHAT ARE SOME OTHER WORDS
THAT DESCRIBE GOD'S STRENGTH?
MY FAVORITE VERSE THIS WEEK WAS...?

_____
_____
_____
_____
_____
_____
_____
_____
_____
_____
_____
_____
_____
_____
_____
_____
_____
_____
_____
_____
_____
_____
_____

Soul

WHEN WE STAND BEFORE JESUS,
IT WON'T MATTER HOW MUCH WE HAVE HERE,
OR HOW GREAT WE WERE HERE.
WHAT WILL MATTER IS WHAT IS IN OUR SOUL.
DO WE LOVE HIM WITH ALL OUR HEART
AND WITH ALL OUR SOUL?

What are some examples of "refreshing"?

- Jumping in a pool on a hot day?
- After school snack?
- Tall glass of lemonade after yard work?
- Cold glass of water after a game?
- Favorite food after studying for a few hours?

Hopefully, I've listed something that connects to you. The point is, during our day we need refreshment. Commonly we associate refreshment with food and drink, because it gives us a physical or mental strength or energy. What about our soul?

THE LAW OF THE LORD IS PERFECT, REFRESHING THE SOUL. THE STATUTES OF THE LORD ARE TRUSTWORTHY, MAKING WISE THE SIMPLE.
PSALM 19:7

David is referring to God's word here. The law of the Lord is perfect. The word of the Lord is perfect, refreshing the soul. Trusting the word of God, being in the word of God, giving time to the word of God makes wise the simple.

God's word evens the playing field for us all. God doesn't care who we are, or what we do. He doesn't care:

- How high we can jump
- How fast we can run
- How strong we are
- If you have a GPA of 3.0 or a 4.0 (but remember, parents probably do. 😊)

God only cares about what's in your soul!
Getting in His word would be a great way to refresh our soul.

MY FAVORITE WAY TO REFRESH MYSELF IS...
WAYS TO REFRESH YOURSELF SPIRITUALLY ARE...

It's all or nothing! Here is a verse that sounds very similar to a previous text where Mark 12:30 was the main focus.

In this verse Moses was speaking to the Israelites before they entered the promised land. He challenged them to faithfully obey the Lord. These were some of his final days. Moses was warning the Isrealites about idolatry... among other things. He called on the new generation to renew the earlier covenant with God that their parents had broken.

Then he said to them:

BUT IF FROM THERE YOU SEEK THE LORD YOUR GOD, YOU WILL FIND HIM IF YOU SEEK HIM WITH ALL YOUR HEART AND WITH ALL YOUR SOUL.
DEUTERONOMY 4:29

All your soul! You see, it all starts there. You can think about it all you want, but until you have it in your soul, you can't feel it.

I refer to it as "soul level" engagement. Once we commit to a soulful relationship with Jesus, it is so much easier to understand how much He loves us. True belief begins in the heart and soul!

Are we all in?

AM I ALL IN? HOW WILL I GET THERE?
IF I AM THERE, HOW DO I STAY THERE?

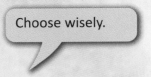

Choose wisely.

DO NOT BE AFRAID OF THOSE WHO KILL THE BODY BUT CANNOT KILL THE SOUL. RATHER, BE AFRAID OF THE ONE WHO CAN DESTROY BOTH SOUL AND BODY IN HELL.
MATTHEW 10:28

Don't be afraid of man, be afraid of God.

A proper fear of God is healthy. He can kill both body and soul in eternal judgment. But... fear of Him overcomes fear of them. God alone controls our eternal destiny. He will welcome us into the Kingdom of Heaven. As believers we will ultimately win the battle over sin and despair.

Believe and share with Him every day of your life. Share your soul with Him. That's what He really wants!

AM I SHARING EVERYTHING WITH JESUS OR JUST THE STUFF I THINK IS SAFE? AM I TRULY PRIORITIZING 15 MINUTES A DAY FOR JESUS?

I go through phases where physical health is important to me. Some of these phases last longer than others. I'll workout or run on a schedule for months. Then I miss a day... then two... then two days become a week... and... well, you get the picture.

I love these personal letters in the second half of the New Testament. John's letter here to Gaius is really neat. His prayer for Gaius is significant. Gaius' spiritual state was so incredible that John prayed his physical health would match his spiritual health.

DEAR FRIEND, I PRAY THAT YOU MAY ENJOY GOOD HEALTH AND THAT ALL MAY GO WELL WITH YOU, EVEN AS YOUR SOUL IS GETTING ALONG WELL.
3 JOHN 1:2

Something that shouldn't be missed... John is praying for balance in Gaius' life. Spiritual health is VERY important!! We all know that. But, it is important for us to take care of our health also. I think some times in our society today this situation is reversed. We can become consumed with our health, and our soul does not get the attention it needs.

Physical health and spiritual health feed off one another. Both are very important to a complete lifestyle.

AM I AS WORRIED ABOUT MY SPIRITUAL HEALTH AS MY PHYSICAL HEALTH?
HOW CAN I MAINTAIN A HEALTHY BALANCE? ☑

We're referring back to Day Two here with the "ALL" reference. But I also wanted to look at two different versions of this verse side by side today to see the subtle differences.

BLESS THE LORD, O MY SOUL: AND ALL THAT IS WITHIN ME, BLESS HIS HOLY NAME.
PSALM 103:1 KJV

PRAISE THE LORD, MY SOUL; ALL MY INMOST BEING, PRAISE HIS HOLY NAME.
PSALM 103:1 NIV

As you can see, the word "bless", when applied to God, means to praise, implying that we always have a strong affection for Him, as well as a sense of gratitude.

The word soul is referring to our heart. Our soul was made to praise Him, to enjoy a relationship with Him, to work toward His perfections.

"All that is within me." All of our energy... our heart, our will, our affections, our emotions. The idea is that God is worthy of all the praise and adoration we can possibly give!

This verse is so simple yet very powerful, and so straightforward with His expectations for us.

AM I ENJOYING A RELATIONSHIP WITH JESUS? HOW AM I SPENDING MY TIME WITH HIM?

Let's talk about choices... think "forks" in the road. Here is an AMAZING verse that refers to that sort of choice.

If you've ever wondered what God wants, spend more time with Jeremiah. He struggled to know God's plan for his life. Even after he "figured it out", outside pressures made him wonder if he had done the right thing. The things he discovered along the way can help us when we feel "stressed out" about serving God during difficult times.

The title in my NIV Bible for this chapter is: Jerusalem Under Siege.

THIS IS WHAT THE LORD SAYS: "STAND AT THE CROSSROADS AND LOOK; ASK FOR THE ANCIENT PATHS, ASK WHERE THE GOOD WAY IS, AND WALK IN IT, AND YOU WILL FIND REST FOR YOUR SOULS. BUT YOU SAID, 'WE WILL NOT WALK IN IT.'"
JEREMIAH 6:16

Here is your visual: Lost travelers are stopping to inquire about the right way to go, which they once knew before they wandered off the path. See Deuteronomy 32:7

These were the proven ways of the people's godly ancestors. Instead of following the proven ways of the Lord, the only paths that could bring rest for their souls, the people were straying into the ways of idolatry. Jeremiah makes several other references to their stubbornness in Jeremiah 18:15 and Jeremiah 23:12.

The path to righteousness is available for each and every one of us. Not everyone finds it. The question is... do we want to find it? I believe with all my heart and soul, that we find it if we want to. Remember something we've discussed before, salvation is not a one time happening, it is a walk through life with Jesus.

The Lord made the path for ALL OF US! When we walk on that path in His light, we find rest for our souls.

WHAT WAS THE BEST PART OF TODAY'S MESSAGE? WE'VE ALL CHOSEN THE WRONG DIRECTION IN OUR LIVES BEFORE. HOW DID I GET BACK ON TRACK?

Have you ever seen a sale sign in a store that says: "As is, no exchanges." That's a risky purchase, right? Even if it is a great price. Well, there won't be any exchanges or bargaining when we get to Heaven either.

WHAT GOOD WILL IT BE FOR SOMEONE TO GAIN THE WHOLE WORLD, YET FORFEIT THEIR SOUL? OR WHAT CAN ANYONE GIVE IN EXCHANGE FOR THEIR SOUL?
MATTHEW 16:26

Our earthly life is temporary. I know 90 years old seems like a LOOONG way off to you... it still seems a long time to me, too.

When it's time to join our Heavenly Father, it won't matter what we have. We can possess all the world's finest things and still be lost, right? In fact, we probably would be lost.

When we stand before Jesus, it won't matter how much we have here or how great we were. What will matter? What is in our soul. Do we love Him with all our heart and with all our soul? Have we asked him for forgiveness? Have we treated others fairly and justly?

You see, it simply comes down to soul level engagement.

SHOULD I MAKE DEALS WITH JESUS? EXAMPLE:
JESUS, I'LL START SPENDING MORE TIME WITH YOU IF
YOU COULD JUST HELP ME GET AN A ON THIS TEST.
WHAT WAS THE MOST IMPACTFUL PART
OF THIS WEEK?

Humility

ARE WE TRULY DEPENDENT ON THE GRACE OF
GOD, FOR OUR SALVATION? ARE WE PREPARED TO
HUMBLE OURSELVES BEFORE HIM?
ARE WE GOING TO SUBMIT TO THE WILL OF GOD?
HE CROWNS THE HUMBLE WITH VICTORY.
HUMBLE FOLLOWERS DEPEND ON THE
GRACE OF GOD FOR THEIR SALVATION.

"I'm so proud of myself! I'm so cool! I'm the Man!!"

What do you think? Am I right? Wait... don't you dare answer that! 😊💪👕🖤

Humility was NOT part of my vocabulary when I was your age. Is it part of yours?

WHEN PRIDE COMES, THEN COMES DISGRACE,
BUT WITH HUMILITY COMES WISDOM.
PROVERBS 11:2

Does this mean we should not be proud of anything we've done? No, of course not. You have lots of accomplishments you can be proud of.

The kind of pride referred to here is arrogance and smug self-satisfaction. An attitude like that is very different than what God expects from us. We have to remember to take those things we have pride in and do them to glorify God. The things we have pride in should never become more important than God.

Godly people can and should take pride in a job well done or in their children as long as they give glory to God for making it ALL possible! 🖤💪👕🙏

HOW HARD IS IT TO BE HUMBLE? ARE THERE TIMES I SHOULD TAKE MORE PRIDE IN WHAT I DO?

Does the Lord take delight in everyone? Although the Lord loves everyone, He is not always happy with everyone. Some are locked in habitual sin and continue their life without Him in it. Certainly He is not happy about that.

But the people who come to Him, seek His strength, ask for His forgiveness, and humble themselves before him, those are the people that He is delighted with.

Are we truly dependent on the grace of God, for our salvation? Are we prepared to humble ourselves before Him? Are we going to submit to the will of God? That is the second half of the verse. He crowns the humble with victory. Humble followers depend on the grace of God for their salvation. That's the victory!

HOW HUMBLE AM I BEFORE GOD?
HAVE I TRULY SUBMITTED TO THE WILL OF GOD?

Serving one another?
Washing feet?
What? Well, OK...

NOW THAT I, YOUR LORD AND TEACHER,
HAVE WASHED YOUR FEET, YOU ALSO
SHOULD WASH ONE ANOTHER'S FEET.
JOHN 13:14

Use your 15 minutes today to read all of John chapter 13. Several valuable lessons here, but most important is humility. Peter needed to understand that Jesus came to serve, not to be served. Peter thought that it was beneath the Messiah to wash feet. It was the perfect time to show the opposite. It's not necessarily about washing feet, it's about serving one another.

This situation exemplifies the spirit of humbleness. Humble acts that all believers should show one another. What can we do?

We can put someone else's needs before ours. We can ask someone who's serving us, "How's your day going?" We can hold the door for someone.

So, being humble and kindness go together... I know we won't be washing anyone's feet, but let's all do one random thing in a humble and kind way today! OK?

WHAT ELSE DID JOHN 13 MAKE ME THINK ABOUT? WHAT CAN I DO TODAY TO SHOW MY HUMILITY?

Are we humble enough to submit to the Lord? I don't want to be too elementary about it, but let's take a quick look at the definitions:

- Humility: A modest view of ones importance.
- Submit: To yield to a superior force.

COME LET US BOW DOWN IN WORSHIP, LET US KNEEL BEFORE THE LORD OUR MAKER.
PSALM 95:6

Is it really that important to understand all that? I believe it is. He is the Creator. He made everything! We are His natural beings and we are supported by Him. We were created by Him, in His image! We should worship Him, both physically and spiritually.

I believe that most people are humble enough to understand that God is greater than we are. But, I don't think most people ultimately submit to the Lord. Are we all humble enough?

HAVE I SUBMITTED 100% OF MY SOUL TO THE LORD? IF I'M NOT THERE, HOW DO I GET THERE?

Does humility help you get along with others? You better believe it!

FINALLY, ALL OF YOU, BE LIKE MINDED, BE SYMPATHETIC, LOVE ONE ANOTHER, BE COMPASSIONATE AND HUMBLE.
1 PETER 3:8

I don't think it is an accident that humble is last on this list. I feel being humble ties the rest of the list together. I certainly don't think we can be compassionate, sympathetic or loving, if we are not humble.

For our relationships to be fruitful, there has to be humility between friends, family members, classmates, co-workers, and any other Christian family connections we may have.

My challenge for each of us today... in that list of different relationships that I just listed, who can we be more humble with and what does that take? I know it's not easy, but we can certainly try. Can't we?

WHAT ARE SOME WAYS I CAN BE MORE HUMBLE?
HOW DOES MY HUMILITY HELP ME
GET ALONG WITH OTHERS? 👐🏽

Last but not least... let's look in James today.

James is writing to believers in Israel. He wrote to warn them about bad habits they had developed and that were undermining what they believed.

Please get your Bible out and read the first 9 verses of John chapter 4. In the first 9 verses he gives 9 commands, then in verse 10 he gives the final command.

HUMBLE YOURSELVES BEFORE THE LORD
AND HE WILL LIFT YOU UP.
JAMES 4:10

You see, the first 9 commands/characteristics make up a humble person. When we are conscious of being in God's presence, the Creator of our entire universe, we need to be humble.

Here again, as we saw yesterday from Peter, humility brings a lot of things together and strengthens our other Christian characteristics.

Humility is hard in a society where being "#1" carries sooo much weight! Well guess what, here's what you want to be #1 at...Make Jesus a priority in your life! Let's Make Him #1! Have an awesome day today.

IF I HONESTLY RANKED WHERE I PUT JESUS IN MY DAY, WHERE WOULD IT BE? HOW IS MY 15 MINUTES A DAY GOING?

It is a lot easier to be humble when we know, understand, and commit to our role.

HE MUST BECOME GREATER; I MUST BECOME LESS.
JOHN 3:30

Obviously John is talking about Jesus here. John had a great understanding of his role in God's plan. Until Jesus became publicly known as the Messiah, all of the attention was on John as he preached, baptized and called upon people to repent. All John's work was in preparation for Jesus. When Jesus' public ministry began, the focus shifted to Him and John received less attention.

John is saying something like: "this is the One that I prepared the way for. Now that he is here, I must step aside and let Him take over." What John means is, the messenger is not as important as the message. As the message arrived, the messengers job was done.

John understood his role!

Check out these other verses:

- Malachi 3:1
- Matthew 11:10
- Luke 3:16.

All do a really cool job connecting the Trinity.

CAN I STEP ASIDE INTENTIONALLY SO THE FOCUS CAN
BE ON SOMEONE ELSE?
IS MY ROLE DIFFERENT WITH DIFFERENT FRIENDS?

Life

JESUS IS THE PATH TO LIFE. HE IS THE WAY, THE TRUTH, AND THE LIFE. WHEN WE CHOOSE THAT PATH AND KEEP JESUS AT THE CENTER OF ALL WE DO, HE FILLS OUR LIVES WITH JOY.

FOR WHOEVER WANTS TO SAVE THEIR LIFE WILL LOSE IT, BUT WHOEVER LOSES THEIR LIFE FOR ME, WILL FIND IT. WHAT GOOD WILL IT BE FOR SOMEONE TO GAIN THE WHOLE WORLD, YET FORFEIT THEIR SOUL. OR WHAT CAN ANYONE GIVE IN EXCHANGE FOR THEIR SOUL?

MATTHEW 16:25-26

That is some really heavy stuff!

Whoever wants to save their life... keep living like they're living... worried about their own self-satisfaction... denying Christ and His Gospel.. continuing to live a life that goes down a one-way street called "Sin avenue"... will expose themselves to the wrath of God. But if we are willing to do life with Jesus... to live our life striving toward righteousness... putting our old life aside and turning it all over to Him... accepting Him as our Lord and Savior... then our heavenly life will be wonderful and spent with Him.

When our judgment day comes, all the money in the whole world will not matter. We cannot buy back our soul! We cannot buy our way to an eternal life. Having "EVERYTHING" here, means "NOTHING!" In the eternal kingdom of God, He wants US, not our stuff! He just wants us! We could possess all the world's stuff and still be lost! It reminds me of the story of the rich man in Luke 12, storing up his wealth, but all God wanted was his soul.

Let's do LIFE with Jesus!

DO I LET SELF SATISFACTION GET IN THE WAY OF MY
TIME WITH JESUS? HOW?
AM I DOING LIFE WITH JESUS?

Gosh, what should I do here? Should I make a left or right turn? Aha... I bet the Bible will tell me something.

YOU MAKE KNOWN TO ME THE PATH OF LIFE; YOU WILL FILL ME WITH JOY IN YOUR PRESENCE, WITH ETERNAL PLEASURES AT YOUR RIGHT HAND.
PSALM 16:11

We have our path shown to us if we want it. The path which leads to the source and center of all life, even God Himself! Jesus is the path to life. He is the way, the truth, and the life. When we choose that path and keep Jesus at the center of all we do, He fills our lives with joy.

Jesus is sitting at the right hand of the Father now. As Christians we will be at the right side of Jesus in heaven.

Our Bible is our GPS system for life! There may be different paths for us all. Ultimately, when we put "home" in as our destination, it is taking us all to the same place.

Let's do life with Jesus!

WHAT DOES MY PATH LOOK LIKE TODAY?
IS IT THE PATH JESUS WANTS ME TO FOLLOW?
DO I KEEP JESUS AT THE CENTER OF MY DECISIONS?

"I am going to try a lot harder to be a good Christian this week. I'm going to do a bunch of good deeds, and that will make me closer to God." Can we be more holy by trying harder?

Let's look at a verse in Hebrews:

MAKE EVERY EFFORT TO LIVE IN PEACE WITH EVERYONE AND TO BE HOLY; WITHOUT HOLINESS NO ONE WILL SEE THE LORD.
HEBREWS 12:14

So, short answer is no. Here's the long answer:

We are declared holy before a perfect God because Jesus paid the price for our sins. He made the ultimate sacrifice. Jesus put us in a position where we can accept God.

How do we demonstrate holiness? We demonstrate holiness as we surrender to the Holy Spirit, shaping our will, our choices and our character to Christ, which brings glory to God.

Peter talked about it in 2 Peter 3:14. Make every effort to be blameless, and indeed, we really should strive for this goal! However, our pursuit of holiness should NOT be an attempt to win brownie points with God. We should strive to live Holy lives to show how thankful we are for the amazing gift He gave us.

Pay close attention to this: When we are living OUR life for God, it will change others around us, because, they will see:

- Our actions.
- Our faith.
- Our joy.
- Our thankfulness.

Remember, being a Christian is really about who you are as a person and not so much about what you do. Do good things because "you are" a Christian, not because you "want to be" a Christian. Make sense?

Let's do life with Jesus!

HAVE I EVER DONE SOMETHING GOOD JUST BECAUSE I THOUGHT IT WOULD BENEFIT ME? HAVE I EVER DONE THAT WITH JESUS?

THE LORD WILL KEEP YOU FROM ALL HARM—HE WILL WATCH OVER YOUR LIFE; THE LORD WILL WATCH OVER YOUR COMING AND GOING BOTH NOW AND FOREVERMORE.

PSALM 121:7-8

This is the gracious assurance for all who put their trust in God. The word "keep" is key here. **He will keep us from all harm and watch over our life!** He will hold on to us. This keeping has no expiration date... it goes forever and ever.

If you go back and read this whole Psalm, verse 1 starts with "I lift up my eyes to the mountains— where does my help come from?" And it ends with this beautiful promise from our Great Protector... our Shepherd who watches our over His flock... protecting us from both harm and evil.

"He will watch over our coming and going both now and forevermore." It reminds me a lot of Psalm 23. Read that scripture from the keeping/protective point of view. "Surely your goodness and love will follow me all the days of my life..." All the days of my life, He will keep me from all harm. All the days of my life. I say, let's do life with Jesus!

DO I TRUST THAT GOD IS WATCHING OVER ME AND KEEPING ME SAFE? WHO ELSE KEEPS ME SAFE IN LIFE?

Should we throw caution to the wind and do whatever the heck we want? Or should we really dial in to this life-book called the Bible?

BE VERY CAREFUL THEN, HOW YOU LIVE—NOT AS UNWISE BUT AS WISE, MAKING THE MOST OF EVERY OPPORTUNITY, BECAUSE THE DAYS ARE EVIL.
EPHESIANS 5:15-16

Live like a wise person. It has nothing to do with being intellectually smart, so even I can do it. (LOL) Make good choices. The opposite of wise is foolish. A fool wanders around on a wide path that leads to destruction.

The believer begins their new life in Christ with all the wisdom necessary to live in a Christian manner, but we must also continue to grow in our wisdom so that we can become even more mature in our journey.

As we learn from David and many others in scripture, believers are not immune to reverting to foolishness. One of the most common foolish moves is not believing in God completely. Believing in God for salvation, but not everything else in life.

It is wise to follow the narrow path of life, that leads to heaven. I say... let's do life with Jesus!

HOW MUCH THOUGHT DO I PUT INTO MY DECISIONS? WHEN DO I LOOK TO THE BIBLE FOR ADVICE?

God has ALWAYS wanted a relationship with us. He wants us to do life with Him. That is why he sent Jesus. I've spent a lot of my personal study time in the Bible looking for connections of the Trinity. It helps me tie it all together. With that in mind, here's a good connection:

WHOEVER BELIEVES IN ME, AS SCRIPTURE HAS SAID, RIVERS OF LIVING WATER WILL FLOW FROM WITHIN THEM.
JOHN 7:38

THE LORD WILL GUIDE YOU ALWAYS; HE WILL SATISFY YOUR NEEDS IN A SUN-SCORCHED LAND AND WILL STRENGTHEN YOUR FRAME. YOU WILL BE LIKE A WELL-WATERED GARDEN, LIKE A SPRING WHOSE WATERS NEVER FAIL.
ISAIAH 58:11

God's word never fails! God's word stands FOREVER! In this passage of John, Jesus was able to call on an ancient promise of scripture and make it immediately available to His followers. My own personal interpretation: Jesus is how God has been asking to be in our lives for thousands of years. Here's how I like to think about it. Maybe you've heard this little nugget before:

- God is the promise maker.
- Jesus is the promise keeper.

So, what do y'all think? Want to do life with Jesus?

WHAT IS TODAY'S CONNECTION BETWEEN THE OLD TESTAMENT AND THE NEW TESTAMENT? HOW CAN IT HELP ME?

You may be too young to look in the mirror at your life, right? Or are you? I think each of us, at any age, or any point in our lives, can look in the mirror and recall:

- Decisions we've made
- Fun days we've had with friends and family
- Sad days
- Happy days
- Days we've laughed so hard our bellies hurt
- Days we've cried so much we thought the hurt would never end

It's all part of our life. It's who we are and we cannot erase any of it. And that's OK!

You know why? Jesus loves us, and lives in us, on each and every one of those days. When we're crying, He is wrapping His arms around us. When we are having that big old belly laugh, He's smiling at us! I promise you! He loves that He is part of us!

AS WATER REFLECTS THE FACE,
SO ONE'S LIFE REFLECTS THE HEART.
PROVERBS 27:19

Use this verse as a reflection point. Sit there, right now, and just close your eyes... think... reflect on the most fun times you've ever had doing life with someone else.

When you look in the water, the reflection is unchangeable. Our physical appearance is what it is. However, we all still have time to change our hearts, if we need to.

My wish for today, is that we all do life with Jesus, FOREVER!!

HOW OFTEN DO I REFLECT ON THE
BIG MOMENTS IN MY LIFE?
HOW DOES MY LIFE REFLECT WHAT IS IN MY HEART?

148

Anger

ANGER BECOMES DESTRUCTIVE
WHEN YOU CAN'T CONTROL IT ANYMORE
AND IT STARTS TO CONTROL YOU.
BEFORE IT BECOMES SIN, JUST LET IT GO.

I'm sure there are times when we get angry a little quicker than normal. Like when we were all on lockdown and couldn't get out as much. Let's look at:

MY DEAR BROTHERS AND SISTERS, TAKE NOTE OF THIS; EVERYONE SHOULD BE QUICK TO LISTEN, SLOW TO SPEAK AND SLOW TO BECOME ANGRY BECAUSE HUMAN ANGER DOES NOT PRODUCE THE RIGHTEOUSNESS THAT GOD DESIRES.
JAMES 1:19-20

Take this one little piece of advice from me... when anger comes suddenly, turn away, put your head down, smile or whatever you need to do to give yourself about 10 seconds. I have worked very hard at this in my own life.

We have been given anger as an emotion. Anger is not necessarily sinful. **Even Jesus got angry.** Anger that leads to rage and revenge is clearly wrong and needs to be handled quickly just to prevent us from doing or saying something that makes things MUCH worse!

Take a deep breath and count to ten. It helps me tremendously. You can also make it part of your prayer Life. Talk to Jesus about it. He wants to help you!

ON A SCALE OF 1 TO 10, WHERE 10 EQUALS "BEING MAD A LOT", I RATE MY ANGER AS...
HOW COULD I GET A BETTER RATING?

> A GENTLE ANSWER TURNS AWAY WRATH,
> BUT A HARSH WORD STIRS UP ANGER.
> **PROVERBS 15:1**

OK, I can be pretty specific in my commentary here because I was this person, many years ago. I was "the guy" who just couldn't leave it alone. A simple misunderstanding that was nothing was made "something" by me, more than once. I am NOT very proud of that.

Always be patient. Please remember that! Just be patient. I'll always ask myself this question...How will what I'm about to do right now look on the front page of the paper tomorrow? If it's not good, just walk away from it.

> A HOT TEMPERED PERSON STIRS UP CONFLICT, BUT
> THE ONE WHO IS PATIENT CALMS A QUARREL.
> **PROVERBS 15:18**

Words and actions can be hurtful and even worse. Think things through; be slow to act. You will never regret patience here. Patience and kindness go a long way. Especially when it may not be the "popular" decision.

The next words that come out of your mouth could hurt a friendship, or even start a fight. Take an extra 15 seconds and think about your response, or better yet, just walk away!

Have a great week!

DO I GET ANGRY ABOUT THE LITTLE THINGS?
ON A SCALE OF 1 TO 10, WHERE 10 EQUALS
"VERY PATIENT", HOW PATIENT AM I?

Anger is a tough emotion. As we look in the Bible, there are times when anger is definitely used against sinful things, and that is a little different. But, for the most part, showing anger just doesn't work out very often...

A QUICK TEMPERED PERSON DOES FOOLISH THINGS, AND THE ONE WHO DEVISES EVIL SCHEMES IS HATED.
PROVERBS 14:17

The first half is obvious, take a breath and think things through. But for the second part of this verse, it gets worse. Have you ever been so angry about something that you actually "planned out" against someone or about something?

WHOEVER IS PATIENT HAS GREAT UNDERSTANDING, ONE WHO IS QUICK TEMPERED DISPLAYS FOLLY.
PROVERBS 14:29

Let's face it, there are times when we have every right to be angry about something. **Having patience is key to keeping it together.** Usually, when we react quickly, things turn out badly.

WHEN CONFRONTED WITH A TOUGH SITUATION THAT
MAKES ME ANGRY, COULD I (SHOULD I) SIT A FEW
MINUTES AND THINK THINGS THROUGH? HAVE I
EVER SENT AN ANGRY TEXT AND REGRETTED IT?

While under house arrest in Rome, Paul wrote to the Colossians. Again, this was one of those situations where there were new believers and they were "under attack" by people who wanted them to believe something different.

YOU USED TO WALK IN THESE WAYS, IN THE LIFE YOU ONCE LIVED. BUT NOW YOU MUST RID YOURSELVES OF ALL SUCH THINGS AS THESE: ANGER, RAGE, MALICE, SLANDER AND FILTHY LANGUAGE FROM YOUR LIPS.
COLOSSIANS 3:7-8

Now, get your Bibles out, since you have to anyway for your 15 minutes today 😊 and read just a little bit further to verse 11.

Paul tells us in verse 8, we have to get these things that tear us apart out of our lives. There is no room for anger. It just weighs us down and causes us to complain and talk bad about other people. It takes up precious time in our lives plotting revenge, etc. Get rid of it.

Then in verse 11, Paul makes sure we are reminded, that **Christ is in EVERY one of us.** Not just certain people, but everyone! Just a A GREAT reminder of the beautiful life we get to live, as we give up the nasty things holding us back!

HOW WOULD TAKING ANGER OUT OF MY LIFE MAKE ME A BETTER PERSON? CAN ANGER HOLD ME BACK FROM A BETTER RELATIONSHIP WITH JESUS?

Anger eats at you, right?

Anger results in so many negative things. Go ahead, look in the mirror and make your mad face. The squinty eyes give you crow's feet and your clenched jaw ruins your bite. Is it really worth it?

Anger ruins relationships and eats up your time because you continue to think about it and just get angrier! That doesn't make any sense. Is it really worth it?

If you've gotten angry about something really silly this week, go look in the mirror and tell yourself that was really silly. **If you've gotten angry with someone this week, call them, work it out.** You will feel so much better.

HAVE I EVER STAYED ANGRY ABOUT SOMETHING FOR DAYS OR WEEKS? WHAT DID IT ACCOMPLISH?

DON'T HAVE ANYTHING TO DO WITH FOOLISH AND
STUPID ARGUMENTS, BECAUSE YOU KNOW THEY
PRODUCE QUARRELS. AND THE LORDS SERVANT
MUST NOT BE QUARRELSOME, BUT MUST BE KIND
TO EVERYONE, ABLE TO TEACH, NOT RESENTFUL.
2 TIMOTHY 2:23-24

Here's another example of Paul giving out some pretty sound advice. Paul is talking to Christians about **not getting caught up in arguments over small differences in core beliefs,** basically quarreling over who is more spiritual.

Apparently the false teachers in Ephesus thrived on debate. Paul warned Timothy not to get caught up in this stuff. But Paul also did not want the Gospel compromised.

We can surely do that today, right? We get involved in an argument or have a fight with a friend, and five days later, we're like "what was that even about?" At the same time, I would hope that we don't let someone else's difference change us, especially our core beliefs.

HAVE I EVER GOTTEN ANGRY ABOUT SOMETHING THAT DOESN'T EVEN MAKE SENSE? 🙁

IN YOUR ANGER, DO NOT SIN. DO NOT LET THE
SUN GO DOWN, WHILE YOU ARE STILL ANGRY,
AND DO NOT GIVE THE DEVIL A FOOTHOLD.
EPHESIANS 4:26

So...Is anger ever okay? Well, if you think about it, anger is a human emotion. God gave it to us. There are times where God and Jesus have been angry. It can be a powerful tool for confronting wrong.

- Exodus 4:14
- Matthew 3:5

Anger at sin, evil, and injustice is a sign of righteousness. But anger that leads to rage and revenge is clearly wrong! Listen... it just clouds your judgment and we end up doing terrible things. Anger really becomes destructive when you can't control it anymore and it starts to control you.

So, "do not let the sun go down" is simply telling us to get over our anger quickly, before it becomes sin. Just let it go.

House/family rule: Never go to bed angry!! NEVER EVER!!!

HOW CAN I SHED MY ANGER QUICKLY BEFORE IT BECOMES SINFUL? HOW DO I FEEL ABOUT THAT HOUSE RULE?

Patience

WE SHOULD TRUST GOD IN CIRCUMSTANCES THAT ARE BEYOND OUR CONTROL. THE PSALM URGES US TO SEE THE WISDOM OF WORKING HARD TO CHANGE WHAT WE CAN BUT TRUSTING GOD WITH WHAT WE CANNOT.

Let's have a little patience my friends! Patience is a pretty good quality to have, but why is it so hard to possess? I think it's because we get excited about "stuff" like birthdays, Christmas, going back to school, etc...

Well once again, in Galatians, Paul was writing to new believers, warning them about false teachers.

LET US NOT BECOME WEARY IN DOING GOOD,
FOR AT THE PROPER TIME WE WILL REAP
A HARVEST IF WE DO NOT GIVE UP.
GALATIANS 6:9

Go back to like verse 5, and look at Paul's advice: Don't compare yourself to other people, take care of your own load

So, what is this "harvest"? The harvest is our eternal life with God and getting to meet Him in heaven. Paul is telling us... no matter what these false teachers tell you, keep fighting, keep spreading the word. That's the good.

Don't become weary of doing those things, because the day will come when we "get to" reap the harvest. Remember that being a Christian is a lot more about who you are as a person than it is about what you do. Who you are creates what you do! Please understand that.

The new believers in Galatia had opportunities to be patient, probably thinking about rewards for their belief. However, they just didn't understand that is not how it works. So, looking at patience 2,000 years ago, it looks a little bit like today. How can we show more patience today, in our own life? Pass it along!

IS IT HARD TO BE PATIENT SOMETIMES? HOW CAN I WORK ON MY OWN PATIENCE?

A PSALM OF DAVID. BE STILL BEFORE THE LORD
AND WAIT PATIENTLY FOR HIM, DO NOT FRET WHEN
PEOPLE SUCCEED IN THEIR WAYS, AND WHEN
THEY CARRY OUT THEIR WICKED SCHEMES.
PSALM 37:7

David's advice here... we should trust God in circumstances that are beyond our control. David urges us to see the wisdom of working hard to change what we can but trusting God with what we cannot.

DOES JESUS SHOW ME PATIENCE?
WHO CAN I BE MORE PATIENT WITH? HOW?

MAY THE GOD WHO GIVES ENDURANCE AND
ENCOURAGEMENT GIVE YOU THE SAME ATTITUDE OF
MIND TOWARD EACH OTHER THAT
CHRIST JESUS HAD.
ROMAN 15:5

So, a lot going on here. As you know Paul wrote Romans. He wanted to encourage the Roman believers to rely solely on God's grace for their salvation, and live transformed lives through Christ. There were lots and lots of disagreements on different things between early Christians. Wow, sound a little like today?

Here's the deal... the goal is not to think exactly alike or to avoid all disagreements. **The goal is to glorify God!** Our different gifts (spiritual gifts) can all combine for greater glory to God.

Paul talks about endurance here as patience to go the distance with our beliefs. When you know the truth, spread it. Share with other believers and non-believers.

AM I PATIENT WITH PEOPLE WHO ARE DIFFERENT? THESE THINGS MAKE ME IMPATIENT...

> THEREFORE, AS GOD'S CHOSEN PEOPLE, HOLY AND
> DEARLY LOVED, CLOTHE YOURSELVES WITH COMPASSION,
> KINDNESS, HUMILITY, GENTLENESS AND PATIENCE.
> **COLOSSIANS 3:12**

Colossian 3 verses 5 and 8, tell us what to avoid, what to stop doing. Here, Paul offers **five ways of life that Christians should follow.**

I love the way he refers to us as God's chosen people. It's like, wow, God really chose me? Yes, He did! Then in the very next line he refers to us as holy, which means set apart. So, God chose us and set us aside.

Since God chose us for this new life of love, we get a new wardrobe, which includes patience. I don't know about you, but I'm pretty sure He wants us to wear the patience "shirt" all the time, right? Not just certain days or with certain people. Showing patience all the time can be VERY difficult. I'm positive you've struggled with it.

Think about our life today... fast food drive-thrus. I mean, we can get food in less than three minutes from order to chewing and still get frustrated with someone over it.

God wants us to have patience. Paul reminds us of it. It's important to work at. Yes! We have to work at it. Think about how patience and last weeks topic of anger go together most of the time. I'm sure you remember the phrase in the Bible "slow to anger". Patience will serve us well in our lives.

CAN I "STOP SCRATCHING THE SCAB"?
AM I SLOW TO ANGER? CAN I DO BETTER?

Here's a great, personal example of patience from me. I had a scab on my leg from a little mishap and it itched like CRAZY! Well, the boo boo needs time to heal, that's why I have a scab. I know that if I scratch the scab off, the healing process is basically going to start all over again. So, what do I do?

My point is this: patience is a part of every aspect of our lives. It does not come naturally to most people. And some people who do possess it, still want to scratch the scab some times. 😊

THE LORD IS NOT SLOW IN KEEPING HIS PROMISE,
AS SOME UNDERSTAND SLOWNESS. INSTEAD
HE IS PATIENT WITH YOU, NOT WANTING ANYONE TO
PERISH, BUT EVERYONE TO COME TO REPENTANCE.
2 PETER 3:9

God wants everyone! All of us. It doesn't matter what age we are or what we've done in our lives. He loves us and wants us to have a relationship with him. How cool is that? All we have to do, is say yes!

He is patient with us, because He knows what's best and has everything all planned out. He is just waiting for us to decide if we want to come to Him or not.

God probably doesn't get impatient waiting on us either. If you think about it, He created the sun and the moon which help us calculate our time, but He measures time factoring in eternity.

HOW HAS GOD SHOWN ME PATIENCE?
HOW DOES IT MAKE ME FEEL WHEN GOD IS PATIENT
WITH ME, EVEN WHEN I'M IMPATIENT WITH OTHERS?

PREACH THE WORD, BE PREPARED IN SEASON
AND OUT OF SEASON, CORRECT, REBUKE AND
ENCOURAGE—WITH GREAT PATIENCE AND
CAREFUL INSTRUCTION.
2 TIMOTHY 4:2

There is a ton of information and instruction for Timothy here in just one verse. It actually takes a lot of patience just to dissect it. 😊

"Be prepared in season", be ready when people who want to hear the word are around. Obviously, it is easier to spread the word to people who want to hear it.

"Out of season," I'm guessing, would be a little more difficult. But, make sure you're ready when it's awkward... or difficult. When people don't believe a word you are saying or even worse... oppose you!

Paul stresses to Timothy to have great patience. How difficult do you think that must have been for Timothy with all the opposition he must have been facing?

Look at Galatians 5:22-23. Paul mentions this as part of the "fruit of the Spirit". He talks about having self control. There are many times in our lives that we need to have and show patience. This example, Paul was kind of telling Timothy... you better be ready for anything! Isn't that true today?

HOW MUCH PATIENCE DID TIMOTHY HAVE TO SHOW?
WHAT DOES IT MEAN TO BE IN AND OUT OF SEASON?

Another message from David:

WAIT FOR THE LORD; BE STRONG AND TAKE HEART AND WAIT FOR THE LORD.
PSALM 27:14

Earlier this week, we talked about God and how He is patient. But what does it mean for "us" to wait for the Lord? Waiting for the Lord is trusting in God's goodness and in His timing. He obviously sees things a little differently than we do.

The answers to our prayers may not always come how we want or as quickly as we want. That is where patience becomes so important. Throughout his life, David waited on God, depending on Him alone for all of his needs.

David discovered the value of patience; he trusted God to send the answer when, and only when, the time was right. You see, it's not about you or me, it's about what God knows is BEST for us!

I saw a great saying and I can't remember where, but it went like this:

"If it's not God's time, you can't force it.
When it is God's time, you can't stop it!"

HOW CAN I TRUST GOD'S GOODNESS AND
TIMING? PATIENCE IS ABOUT LETTING GO AND
UNDERSTANDING GOD IS IN CONTROL...
HOW CAN I ENSURE MY LIFE REFLECTS THAT?

Faith

SIMPLY PUT, FAITH IS TRUSTING GOD AND HOW PEOPLE ACCESS THE SALVATION GOD HAS PROVIDED IN CHRIST JESUS. OUR FAITH IS STRENGTHENED BY PAYING CAREFUL ATTENTION TO THE BIBLE AND PRACTICING THE SPIRITUAL DISCIPLINES.

What is faith? Have you ever been asked that question? It's an important one. How did you answer it? Hebrews 11 tells us a lot about faith, and the first verse explains it pretty well.

NOW FAITH IS CONFIDENCE IN WHAT WE HOPE FOR AND ASSURANCE ABOUT WHAT WE DO NOT SEE.
HEBREWS 11:1

Simply put, faith is trusting God and how people access the salvation God has provided in Christ Jesus. Our faith is strengthened by paying careful attention to the Bible and practicing the spiritual disciplines.

FAITH COMES FROM HEARING THE MESSAGE, AND THE MESSAGE IS HEARD THROUGH THE WORD ABOUT JESUS.
ROMANS 10:17

We trust God to give what he has promised. It might be the gifts and abilities to do the work of Jesus in the world. It can also be what carries us through our spiritual journey and our growth in Him. Faith helps us help others in their journey. Faith is tied to our active trust in God and His word.

HOW WOULD I ANSWER THE
"FAITH" QUESTION BEFORE TODAY?
DID TODAY'S READING CHANGE MY UNDERSTANDING?
DO I ACTIVELY TRUST GOD AND HIS WORD?

_____
_____
_____
_____
_____
_____
_____
_____
_____
_____
_____
_____
_____
_____
_____
_____
_____
_____

Can we please God without having faith? This could be a LONG answer! Let's stay in Hebrews today:

AND WITHOUT FAITH IT IS IMPOSSIBLE TO PLEASE GOD, BECAUSE ANYONE WHO COMES TO HIM MUST BELIEVE THAT HE EXISTS AND THAT HE REWARDS THOSE WHO EARNESTLY SEEK HIM.
HEBREWS 11:6

Here's the deal; without faith, it is impossible to walk with God or please Him. He is the true God. Genuine faith does not simply believe that a divine being exists, but that the God of scripture is the one and only true God.

Look at 1 John 5:10 WOW!! Just WOW!! This may be one of the most important statements in the Bible. If we do not believe in Jesus then how can He possibly be our Savior?

There are many scriptures that talk about how important it is to seek God. He is available to anyone who seeks Him and has faith in Him. He will not force himself on us; you must accept Him of your own free will.

Matthew 7:7 explains it well. Salvation through Jesus Christ is a free gift. The only way to have any gift is to reach out and take it. Salvation must be received through our faith.

DO I SEEK GOD ON A DAILY BASIS
OR JUST WHEN I NEED HIM?
WHAT DOES THE FREE GIFT MEAN TO ME?

ASK AND IT SHALL BE GIVEN TO YOU; SEEK
AND YOU SHALL FIND; KNOCK AND THE
DOOR SHALL BE OPENED FOR YOU.
MATTHEW 7:7

Can our faith be useless? Let's see what Paul has to say about faith in 1 Corinthians:

NOW, BROTHERS AND SISTERS, I WANT TO REMIND YOU OF THE GOSPEL I PREACH TO YOU, WHICH YOU RECEIVED AND ON WHICH YOU HAVE TAKEN YOUR STAND. BY THIS GOSPEL YOU WERE SAVED, IF YOU HOLD FIRMLY TO THE WORD I PREACHED TO YOU. OTHERWISE, YOU HAVE BELIEVED IN VAIN.
1 CORINTHIANS 15:1-2

Yes, our faith can be useless. Part of our faith is the acknowledgment of the facts of the gospel. But it can't simply stop there. Our faith can't be an emotional response that is soon forgotten. Paul was stating the importance of a sincere commitment to Jesus. We have to stay in relationship with Him. If we do not believe that Jesus was raised from the dead our faith is groundless. The resurrection, to Paul's way of thinking, justified Jesus and His message. Faith would be useless without it.

IS FAITH A CONSISTENT, DAILY PRESENCE IN MY LIFE?
HOW CAN I STAY IN CONSTANT CONTACT WITH JESUS?
HOW IS MY 15 MINUTES A DAY GOING? ✌️

BUT YOU, DEAR FRIENDS, BY BUILDING YOURSELVES UP IN YOUR MOST HOLY FAITH AND PRAYING IN THE HOLY SPIRIT, KEEP YOURSELVES IN GOD'S LOVE AS YOU WAIT FOR THE MERCY OF OUR LORD JESUS CHRIST TO BRING YOU TO ETERNAL LIFE.

JUDE 1:20-21

Is praying tied to our faith? How so? We've talked a lot about prayer. We've discussed what to pray about, where to pray, and how often and how long to pray. Most importantly, we've discussed that we all have to understand that prayer is a two-way conversation between us and God.

True believers have a sure foundation. The strength of that foundation is largely determined by the strength of their faith.

URGENT NOTICE

We are each responsible for our own faith.

We may have some spiritual partners who help us along, but...it is OUR obligation to build our faith!

The best way to do that is through prayer and using our faith. The more we use our faith, the more it grows. This is not a call to you for some elaborate form of prayer, simply a call to pray more consistently to build our faith.

DO I EVER HAVE A HARD TIME PRAYING...
OR DECIDING WHAT TO PRAY ABOUT...
OR FIGURING OUT HOW OR WHEN TO PRAY?

When should we be satisfied in our life? Can we ever really be happy, and stop looking for what's next? "I need to make more money, I want a bigger house, I want a better car," these are all things you may think about in the future. What does Paul have to say about all of this?

BUT GODLINESS WITH CONTENTMENT IS GREAT GAIN. FOR WE BROUGHT NOTHING INTO THE WORLD, AND WE CAN TAKE NOTHING OUT OF IT. BUT IF WE HAVE FOOD AND CLOTHING WE WILL BE CONTENT WITH THAT.
1 TIMOTHY 6:6-8

I'm sure you are nodding your heads because you already know this... but it is not how much we have or how important we are that will make us happy. It is our attitude toward life and having Jesus!

If we put our FAITH and trust in the Lord, Jesus Christ, we should be content knowing that whatever is happening to us is for our good. Following Jesus is VERY profitable! Having Jesus in our life will make us so rich! Godliness is not profitable in a financial sense, but following Jesus will give us a piece-of-mind type of contentment.

So, you see... having faith that He is going to provide us with everything we need...IS EVERYTHING WE NEED!!!

HOW IS MY ATTITUDE TOWARD LIFE IN GENERAL?
WHAT ABOUT SCHOOL OR WORK?
TODAY'S READING HELPED ME ...

How can we strengthen our faith? Have you ever heard the phrase "practice makes perfect"? I know it's a tough phrase because we can't be perfect, but we can get better.

FOR IN THE GOSPEL THE RIGHTEOUSNESS OF GOD IS REVEALED—A RIGHTEOUSNESS THAT IS BY FAITH FROM FIRST TO LAST, JUST AS IT IS WRITTEN: "THE RIGHTEOUS WILL LIVE BY FAITH."
ROMANS 1:17

"Righteousness" is doing what is right, obeying God's Law, and adhering to morals.

We know the definition. We know what it requires, yet still we fall short. We still can't get there! As sinful people, how can we be made right with God?

We need to be in relationship with Him. After all, he created us for a relationship with Him. He took the initiative to make the relationship right. He gave us Jesus, whose life was given in exchange for ours. I think as we begin to understand our brokenness we grow deeper in understanding and we grow closer to him. We strengthen our faith by being in relationship with Him.

Practice makes perfect? We can't be perfect, but how often do we still strive for perfection in our lives? in what area do you practice for perfection?

- Sports
- Dance routine
- Grades
- Playing an instrument
- ACT scores
- For our friends
- Can you think of more?

WHAT AM I DOING TO STRENGTHEN MY RELATIONSHIP WITH JESUS? WILL I CHANGE WHAT I TRY TO BE PERFECT AT?

_____
_____
_____
_____
_____
_____
_____
_____
_____
_____
_____

Why do we not strive for that same perfection in our relationship with Jesus? Why aren't we consistently spending time with Him? The crazy part about it is, we don't even have to be perfect for Him. He already knows our issues and still wants us! Why don't we practice with Him every day?

I'm wondering how much time it would take every day to strengthen our faith, by checking in with Him... let's try 15, minutes maybe?

Can you "see" Faith? Well... you should be able to!

IF YOU DECLARE WITH YOUR MOUTH, "JESUS IS THE LORD," AND BELIEVE IN YOUR HEART THAT GOD RAISED HIM FROM THE DEAD, YOU WILL BE SAVED. FOR IT IS WITH YOUR HEART THAT YOU BELIEVE AND ARE JUSTIFIED, AND IT IS WITH YOUR MOUTH THAT YOU PROFESS YOUR FAITH AND ARE SAVED.

ROMANS 10:9-10

Salvation comes by faith but faith is NOT just knowledge of the facts. I believe that genuine faith can be seen in our actions. The presence of faith can be seen in a loving relationship with God.

Even though sin broke this relationship, God provided Jesus to bring us back together. We are saved when we believe Jesus died and was resurrected, and when we sincerely trust in Him as our only way to eternal life.

Our convictions will eventually be visible by our words and how we are living our life. Today's verse would be a yellow rope moment! How visible is your faith in Jesus Christ?

CAN PEOPLE SEE MY FAITH BY MY ACTIONS?
HOW VISIBLE IS MY RELATIONSHIP
WITH JESUS TO OTHERS?

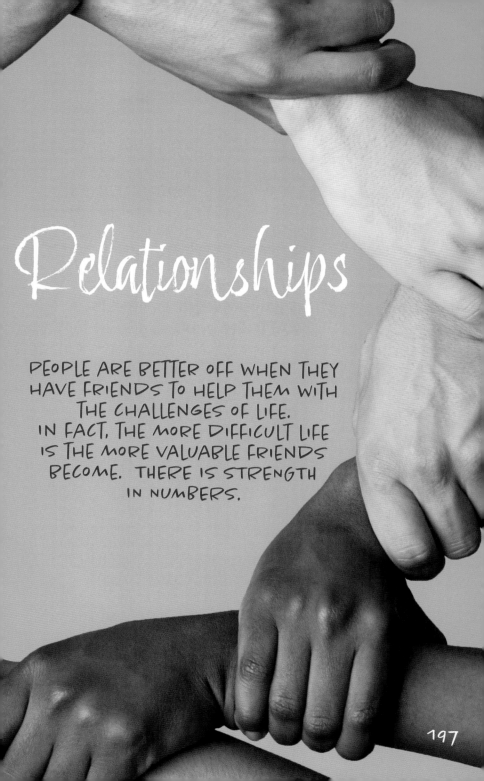

Relationships

PEOPLE ARE BETTER OFF WHEN THEY
HAVE FRIENDS TO HELP THEM WITH
THE CHALLENGES OF LIFE.
IN FACT, THE MORE DIFFICULT LIFE
IS THE MORE VALUABLE FRIENDS
BECOME. THERE IS STRENGTH
IN NUMBERS.

"Is that the way you want to be treated? What if Mark did that to you? How would you like it if...? If you're not nice to other people then...?"

Relationships...
- They can be easy.
- They can be difficult.

We've heard those statements or some version of them hundreds of times. Relationships can be easy and they can be difficult, too. Of course, we know THE GOLDEN RULE, RIGHT!?

SO IN EVERYTHING, DO TO OTHERS WHAT YOU WOULD HAVE THEM DO TO YOU, FOR THIS SUMS UP THE LAW AND THE PROPHETS.
MATTHEW 7:12

So, treat people the way you want to be treated. Gosh, who hasn't needed to hear that little piece of advice?
It may be the most common thing that we've heard over the years. Let's see, who's told us that?

- Parents
- Teachers
- Coaches

We see a few different versions of the same basic message in several areas of the Bible. After doing my research, I've discovered that versions of the "Golden Rule" existed before Jesus. However, all of them cast the rule as a negative command. One version by Rabbi Hillel goes, "What is hateful to yourself do not to someone else."

Jesus made it a positive command, enriching its meaning to do good. Be nice to other people. Treat people fairly. Don't judge. Love everyone! Do all those things NO MATTER WHAT! 😊

We should expect the same kind of treatment we give. Giving is very much a part of receiving and that's tough sometimes because it can play out several different ways. We don't always get it right, but there are times where we do treat others really nice and we don't get the same in return. There are times where we mess up and we get the same treatment. There are times where we mess up and the other person gets it right. When that happens to me, I really feel like a terrible person. 😞

When relationships and general interactions are genuine and nice, our world is a beautiful place! This week, let's strive for perfect execution of THE GOLDEN RULE. Have a great week!

THESE ARE THE TOUGHEST RELATIONSHIPS IN MY LIFE... WHAT MAKES THEM DIFFICULT? HOW CAN I HELP CHANGE THEM? DO I LIVE BY "THE GOLDEN RULE"?

"There's strength in numbers!" You've heard that before, right?

Let's look at the Bible for scripture that speaks to strength in numbers. We are going to Ecclesiastes. According to tradition, Solomon is the author of this book, though many historians now doubt that. Some believe it was an unnamed teacher or leader who played the role of a king. No matter who the author, the book offers valuable advice.

THOUGH ONE MAY BE OVERPOWERED, TWO CAN DEFEND THEMSELVES, A CORD OF THREE STRANDS IS NOT QUICKLY BROKEN.
ECCLESIASTES 4:12

"The teacher" was obviously practical. If you read this chapter from the beginning, you'll see he was talking about a corrupt world full of troubles. So, here he is in the middle of all that, suggesting one way of coping: people are better off when they have friends to help them with the challenges of life. In fact, the more difficult life is the more valuable friends become. THERE IS STRENGTH IN NUMBERS!

Think about the last part of today's verse "a cord of three strands is not quickly broken." Think about a braided rope. That's why there's 2 or 3 ropes made in to one, right? FOR STRENGTH!

Well it's the same thing with relationships. They bring us strength. Here's an assignment for today! Reach out to at least one person, who you are grateful to be "doing life with", and tell them that. Say it out loud! Tell them how thankful you are for their companionship.

HOW MANY PEOPLE ARE IN MY CIRCLE OF TRUE FRIENDS? CAN THEY COUNT ON ME? DO WE SHARE JESUS WITH EACH OTHER?

If really think about it, you have to be a good person if you want good people to hang out with, just as you should be seeking good people to hang out with. Not always the popular choice, I get it.

I grew up in a small town. Population was about 2,100. I couldn't get away with anything! EVERYONE knew my dad and they all knew I was Jack Hikes' kid. My dad was not a man of many words, but when he spoke, I listened! One of his more serious pieces of advice/threat: 🖤💪

"Mark, don't ever do anything to ruin our good name. I've always tried to treat people right and do the right thing. People appreciate and respect that. Please don't ever do anything to take away from that."

As I got older, I could see that and understand his wishes. Having a good name was very important to him. And guess what... to this day, when I go back, I can't get through town without hearing: "Hey, you're Jack Hikes' boy right?" Followed by, "Your dad was:

- A really good man
- A great friend
- Always there to help me
- Always smiling

Believe it or not, that is a lot to live up to. Trust me, I was pretty straight and narrow but made a few mistakes. 😊

So, let's bring some wisdom into the relationship theme with Proverbs 22:1:

A GOOD NAME IS MORE DESIRABLE THAN GREAT RICHES; TO BE ESTEEMED IS BETTER THAN SILVER OR GOLD.
PROVERBS 22:1

I'm sure God was smiling down on my dad, EVERY time I got that line. So, how can a person acquire a good name? In a sense this is what Proverbs is all about. A good name develops from the pursuit and practice of wisdom, making good choices, and maintaining good RELATIONSHIPS!

Wise people earn a good reputation as they learn to live a good life... treating others with respect... making good decisions... and showing a genuine concern for others. Riches such as gold and silver are not permanent, maybe nice to have, but not nearly as important as more permanent things. The good name of a family will help children and grandchildren for a very long time. I certainly got an opportunity or two in my life because of who my father was. 😊

I like to think about all of this in my relationship with Jesus. Jesus has the BEST name EVER. I want to live my life to uphold that! Always remember what others have done before you, it will help you in your relationships today.

HOW DO THE CHOICES I MAKE, LET OTHERS DOWN? DOES THAT CHANGE THE DECISIONS I MAKE?

FOR THIS VERY REASON, MAKE EVERY EFFORT TO ADD TO YOUR FAITH GOODNESS; AND TO GOODNESS, KNOWLEDGE, AND TO KNOWLEDGE, SELF CONTROL; AND TO SELF CONTROL, PERSEVERANCE; AND TO PERSEVERANCE, GODLINESS; AND TO GODLINESS, MUTUAL AFFECTION; AND TO MUTUAL AFFECTION, LOVE.
2 PETER 1:5-7

There are quite a few good relationship characteristics in those verses. Having FAITH will help in relationships. Hopefully we all attract or have other people of faith in our company. Having GOODNESS... an overall good person is the type of person I want to be around. Sometimes we need self control in our relationships, because something might not be our business or we need to just let stuff go. Perseverance will help us get through tough times in our relationships.

Godliness will most certainly benefit us in relationships. I can't tell you how many times I'm in a situation and I say out loud, 'That was not very Christ Like". It may be about myself or about another person. I'll group mutual affection and love together. Obviously there is some sort of mutual affection when we have a relationship with someone. You have to like each other, whether it is friendship or romantic, then having love for someone else is HUGE. To me, it's the deepest level of connection/ commitment.

I have probably 5 guy friends that I say "I love you" to when we leave each other's presence or hang up the phone. It's my way of telling that person "hey, I really care about you and what happens to you." Take a few minutes today and think about those relationship characteristics. What ones do you need to work on? What are your strengths?

DO I MAINTAIN GOOD RELATIONSHIPS WITH MY FRIENDS? WHAT ABOUT JESUS? HOW CAN TODAY'S READING HELP ME?

So, should we limit ourselves to relationships only with fellow believers? What a great question! Let's start with a few verses from Paul's second letter to the Corinthians:

DO NOT BE YOKED TOGETHER WITH UNBELIEVERS. FOR WHAT DO RIGHTEOUSNESS AND WICKEDNESS HAVE IN COMMON? OR WHAT FELLOWSHIP CAN LIGHT HAVE WITH DARKNESS? WHAT HARMONY IS THERE BETWEEN CHRIST AND BELIAL? OR WHAT DOES A BELIEVER HAVE IN COMMON WITH AN UNBELIEVER?
2 CORINTHIANS 6:14-15

Belial is a Hebrew word used to characterize the worthless and the wicked.

Paul was not saying that Christians must avoid unbelievers. Avoiding relationships with unbelievers would defy the purpose that God has for us. He was saying that Christians should avoid the kinds of associations that will cause us to adopt their values and patterns of behavior.

After all, Jesus associated with sinners in order to show God's love on them, but He influenced them rather than adopting their values. Again... it's all about the RELATIONSHIPS we form! As Jesus followers, we are to be the salt and light in this world, sharing God's goodness and truth with EVERYONE. EVERYONE! Share with believers, unbelievers, people of all backgrounds. We may learn as much from someone as we give, if we just listen.

Sharing is a two way street. Relationships are NOT meant to be one way streets.

WHAT ARE "RELATIONSHIP CHARACTERISTICS"?
ON A SCALE OF 1 TO 10, WHERE 10 EQUALS "BEST",
HOW DO I RATE MYSELF ON TODAY'S
RELATIONSHIP CHARACTERISTICS?

God or man? You choose! Should we choose? Do we have to choose?

AM I NOW TRYING TO WIN THE APPROVAL OF HUMAN BEINGS, OR OF GOD? OR AM I TRYING TO PLEASE PEOPLE? IF I WERE STILL TRYING TO PLEASE PEOPLE, I WOULD NOT BE A SERVANT OF CHRIST.
GALATIANS 1:10

Go back and read the beginning of the chapter. Critics were accusing Paul of teaching an "easy gospel" to increase his popularity. They thought that faith alone, without the Jewish law, was a watered down gospel. They had been following all these laws forever! Paul's concern was simply for spiritual truth, not about his approval ratings.

That's a great example where relationships might get a little tough. Paul had one message and he was right. That's all he cared about. He obviously added to his sincerity by telling the story of his own conversion. The most compelling evidence of his teaching was his own dramatic conversion from a violent enemy of the church, to the church's most active missionary. Jesus said we can determine who is telling the truth by observing the persons life and the fruit he or she produces. What fruit do we bring to our RELATIONSHIPS?

It would have been easy for Paul to throw in the towel, but he didn't. Why not? Because of his RELATIONSHIP with Jesus! His relationship with Jesus was too important to him. Paul chose Jesus over man. How important is our relationship with Jesus to us?

DO I SHARE JESUS WITH MY FRIENDS? DO I HAVE FRIENDS WHO DON'T REALLY TALK ABOUT JESUS? IS IT BECAUSE THEY DON'T BELIEVE OR WE ARE UNSURE HOW TO BRING HIM UP? ✌🏻🖤✝️

Relationships have a lot to do with love we have for one another. ♥

MAY THE LORD MAKE YOUR LOVE INCREASE AND OVERFLOW FOR EACH OTHER AND EVERYONE ELSE, JUST AS OURS DOES FOR YOU.
1 THESSALONIANS 3:12

The type of love spoken of here is the unselfish love God has for all mankind. He loves us even when we are unlovable. If we have taken on the name Christian (Christ-like), then we must have that unselfish love for every single person on the planet just like Jesus does. Read Mark 12:30-31.

LOVE THE LORD YOUR GOD WITH ALL YOUR HEART AND WITH ALL YOUR SOUL AND WITH ALL YOUR MIND AND WITH ALL YOUR STRENGTH. THE SECOND IS THIS: 'LOVE YOUR NEIGHBOR AS YOURSELF.' THERE IS NO COMMANDMENT GREATER THAN THESE.
MARK 12:30-31

God loves us despite our faults, asking nothing in return except that we believe in Him. We must learn to build relationships by learning to love the same way God loves us!

WHAT THINGS HAVE I LEARNED FROM THIS BOOK? HOW HAS IT MADE ME CLOSER TO JESUS?

PUBLISHER'S CORNER

Each time we publish a book, the author and I spend a good bit of time together during the production process. We form relationships that sometimes become lifetime friendships. Mark and I have definitely formed this lifetime connection, and it all started the first time I met him.

The production team was scheduled to meet with a potential new author. Mark walks in my home and immediately has this air of bewilderment. He's looking all around, and I'm thinking maybe he thinks he's in the wrong place. As I walk toward him and extend my hand to introduce myself, he just says, "Who lives here?"

I'm about tell him my husband and I live here, and in walks Roger from the back. Mark's face lights up. "It's you!" Seems Roger and Mark had met previously and had a long talk about Jesus. The relationship had begun, and I didn't even know it yet.

Editing and laying out *15 Minutes with Jesus* has been life altering. Mark has an amazing way of reminding me that Jesus is about relationship. It's not about being perfect. It's not about coming to him when I feel worthy or when I truly need something. No. It is (or certainly should) be like hanging out with a friend... an amazingly perfect friend who always knows what I need.

I like to tease Mark by saying I never planned to publish his book... because it's true. 😊 We publish mostly cookbooks. Though I have always planned to produce (and maybe even write) a devotional one day, the timing didn't feel right.

I was wrong. To be honest, it was out of my control. Not only did this book have to be published, I had to read it, and then I had to publish it. It's one of those God-things Mark is so fond of talking about.

Through Jesus, we (you and I) have the power to change the world. Mark is doing his part through this book and his amazing ministry. I am so thankful for him.

Sheila Simmons,
Publisher

LET THE WORDS OF MY MOUTH AND THE MEDITATION
OF MY HEART BE ACCEPTABLE UNTO THY SIGHT,
O LORD, MY STRENGTH AND MY REDEEMER.
PSALM 19:14

Thank you for reading the book. My hope is that it will bring you closer to our Father. We should all really try to spend more time with Him! I would love to hear what you think about *15 Minutes with Jesus*. What was your favorite topic? What did it make you think about? How did it make you feel? Did it help you in some way? If so, how?

Feel free to call me or shoot me at text or email:

- **Phone: (717) 439-8575**
- **Email: mhhikes@gmail.com**

ABOUT THE AUTHOR

Mark Hikes lives in Madison, Mississippi, with his wife, Natalie, and two sons, DJ and Jack. They share life with four rescue animals—three dogs, Yetti (Akita), Emma (Australian Shepherd), Maggie (Red Bone Coon Hound), and one cat, Charlie.

Mark lived most of his life in Central Pennsylvania where he was born and raised in the town of Pine Grove. He loves outdoor sports and discipleship time with family and small groups.

Mark is a member of Madison United Methodist Church where he serves as a Family Group Leader.

ACKNOWLEDGMENTS

I am humbled and thankful to have so many people in my life that have inspired me, held me accountable, guided me, and shared in my journey with Jesus.

Jim Genesse, you were my initial conduit to Jesus. I remember the first day I visited MUMC. When you delivered your sermon that day, I felt like I was the only person in the congregation. The scripture reading that day was I Chronicles chapter 16. Verse 11 is still my favorite. You certainly have encouraged me to seek His face always. We have laughed together, and cried with one another. I'm grateful for your guidance over the years, and thankful to call you my friend.

Barry Male, thank you for your constant encouragement, your feedback, and your time. I'm thankful that we have a leader like you in our church. You always manage to expand my ability to comprehend scripture, no matter what my question is. You are never too busy to take my call, and always make time for me, when I stop by the office. That means a lot to me my friend.

Randy Hierlmeier, if it wasn't for you, this book probably never would have happened. You just wouldn't stop telling me that more people needed to see it! Thank you for pushing me, and encouraging me. You ultimately gave me the confidence to show the information to a publisher. I'm so grateful you did.

Cory Phillips, I remember the day you asked if I had thought about being part of the youth program. I wasn't sure at first. It seems odd to even say that out loud now, because being part of our youth program has been such an incredible part of my walk with Christ. Helping the students grow has helped my growth. Thank you for asking me to be part of the team.

Liz Pritchard & Doug Owens, I'm so thankful to share in the student mentoring process with you. Being teamed up with the two of you is a tremendous honor. I love sharing with y'all, and I'm thankful that I get to do life with two people who are excited about walking with the students. You make it a lot of fun. Thank you for the passion and honesty you share with me.

Bob Stanley, We all experience things like doubt or lack of patience in our Christian journey. I remember the day we talked by the pool, and I was frustrated because I just couldn't figure out what it was that Jesus had in store for me. You listened to my confusion and reminded me, "Not everything is going to happen on your time frame. You will know what He wants you to do, on His time frame. You won't know until He knows, be ready for it." You were so right! That was exactly what I needed to hear that day. Thank you for your friendship!

Kevin Partridge, our friendship started with a conversation about our faith and just never stopped! In fact, one of the things I share with others about our friendship is that EVERY time we are together, we talk about Jesus. That is so important to me. You constantly challenge me to think deeper and push to be better. You have helped me understand so much about our relationship with Jesus. You've made me a better disciple. Thank you!

Ben Butler, thank you for sharing "Invitation" with me. Doing that book study with you was a huge part of my journey. It increased my knowledge, and brought me closer to Jesus. Our sharing meetings were, and are still, special to me. I refer back to that book and specific time we spent together often to guide me through the things that I accomplish today. Thank you for your friendship.

Great American Publishers, thank you for giving me this opportunity. From the first day we met, you've made me feel like part of your family. Each and every one of you are incredible. Thank you for your hard work and dedication in putting this book together. I love you so much, I think we should do it again.

The group I have acknowledged here mean so much to me. In different ways, each of them have poured in to me. They have encouraged me, but also challenged me. They have answered many questions, but they are also great listeners. Every one of them spends time with me on my path. All of them have influenced me in different ways. All of you have helped strengthen my relationship with our Father.

Thank you.
I love each and every one of you!

What's next?

First, let me say thank you for reading *15 Minutes with Jesus*. As you know, this book was compiled from a group text we share. The text started as a way for me to stay connected to the students, with the hope that they would grow closer to Jesus. I wanted to give them a daily thought that they could carry through their day, as part of a weekly theme, to help build a consistent relationship with our Shepherd. I hope that it has helped you too.

The text is still going strong every day. As I continue to pick themes, or ask the students to pick them, I find myself wanting

to get just a little more in depth, and focusing a little more on what our relationship with Jesus and others looks like.

In other words, once you are growing with Jesus in your own relationship, it is a great time to share Jesus with someone else. You might simply spend some time in conversation with Christian friends, or you may end up sharing Jesus with someone who doesn't have a relationship with Him.

It's time to share! Are you up for the challenge?

Here's what I want you to always remember; anytime we engage in worship together it is an opportunity to learn, teach and share.

> Therefore go and make disciples of all nations, baptizing them in the name of the Father and of the Son and of the Holy Spirit, and teaching them to obey everything I have commanded you. And surely I am with you always, to the very end of the age.
>
> Matthew 28:19-20

This conversation between Jesus and the disciples, which happened more than 2,000 years ago, is still important for us today. You know why? Because the expectations that He gave to the disciples that day, are the same expectations that He has for us today. Can you imagine what our world would be like, if we all spent 15 minutes a day with Jesus? We've got so much work to do to grow the Christian community, but if we all spend just a little more time focusing our lives on Jesus, we'll get there together. We better get started!

Mark Hikes, Author

Be on the lookout for,
The Next 15 Minutes:
Share Jesus with a Friend.

Great American Publishers

Great American Publishers (Lena, MS) is a small press specializing in souvenir cookbooks.

Our tradition of preserving America's favorite recipes is celebrated in our state cookbook series. The STATE HOMETOWN COOKBOOK SERIES is a hometown taste of America featuring favorite recipes from home cooks along with sidebars about each state's fun food festivals.

The STATE BACK ROAD RESTAURANT RECIPES SERIES is a fun restaurant road trip featuring favorite recipes from chefs and restaurant owners along with profiles about the best locally owned restaurants to enjoy while traveling the state.

In addition to these two series and more, we publish a line of national favorite cookbooks, state specific notebooks, and Christian devotionals.

Call us toll-free for more information
1-888-854-5954

Visit us online
www.GreatAmericanPublishers.com

Connect with us on facebook
www.facebook.com/GreatAmericanPublishers